THE NEXT BIG THING

The Rise, and Inevitable Fall, of Political Programmes

by

Chris West

'Initium ut esset, homo creatus est.'

('Humanity was created to make new things')

St Augustine

To Gervas, who believed in this project from the start

Copyright © 2022 by Chris West

Published by CWTK Publications

Cover design by 100covers

Contents

What is a Political Programme? 1
The Model behind the Model 15
The Life-Cycle of a Political Programme 25
The Model in Action 57
    New Liberalism 60
    Lloyd George's Programmes 70
    Tranquillity 79
    1945 Socialism 91
    Fifties Conservatism 101
    White Heat 111
    The 1970s 122
    Thatcherism 131
    New Labour 144
    The Coalition 155
    Populist 'Brexit' Nationalism 159
    The Next Big Thing? 172
And meanwhile… 182
Ten Quick Tips for the Ambitious 188
Appendices 191
    The Status of the Model 193
    The Big New Ideas 195
    Glossary 198
    UK elections, 1906 to 2019 204
Acknowledgements 207

History tells us, loud and clear, that victory in British politics goes to parties with Big New Ideas. Strategy, not tactics; innovation, not triangulation; a daring, full-on 'Political Programme' – that is how to win, and win big.

There have been ten such Programmes since 1906. This book will tell their individual stories.

It will also model the life-cycle that underlies each one of those stories. Our mediaeval ancestors talked of a wheel of fortune, but they could have been talking about modern politics. This book will show *how* that wheel turns, lifting the fortunate few to great heights but inexorably swinging on round and pulling them back down again –then, of course, starting all over again, with new passengers on board.

It will go on to suggest a Big New Idea for the future – but will do so with caution. The endless turn of the wheel is reassuringly predictable, but what and who flourishes at any given turn is not predictable at all and never can or should be.

As a by-product, the book will provide a defence of Britain's current, often-criticized system of 'representative' democracy. It will show how that system makes original ideas fight hard for expression, then gives the winning ones time and space to be properly actioned, then (perhaps most important of all) lets voters peacefully remove the idea's proponents once their time has passed – for good. Once they are gone, former Programme Leaders may comment in the media or earn fortunes on the speaker circuit, but they no longer run our lives. Neither the authoritarianism currently being touted by Russia and China, nor 'direct democracy', where policy is decided by a series of referenda, allows these things.

I hope that my model will prove a useful guide to the current political scene. Why do the Conservatives seem to have such control over the political narrative, when not long ago they were seen as unelectable dinosaurs in a new, liberal world? Why is the once all-conquering Labour Party still struggling? What ever happened to the Lib Dems? Where are the Greens?

My biggest hope for it, though, is that it will help ambitious future change-makers clamber onto the wheel and realize their hopes and dreams for a better world – for a while, anyway.

What is a Political Programme?

As I say in the strapline to the book's title, this book models The Rise, and Inevitable Fall, of Political Programmes. So, what is a Political Programme?

I define it as:

> A Politically Successful set of Models, Values, Stories and Core Policies, grouped around a Big New Idea.

Let's take this rather scary-looking definition to bits.

Politically Successful
By this, I mean that a Political Programme achieves legislative and executive power, and keeps that power for a decent length of time. In parliamentary politics, this means that it achieves a substantial majority.

One could argue that a movement like feminism has been Politically Successful – it has certainly outlasted any administration, and its influence is felt in all areas of national life. However, this book is about the specific business of creating and then executing government policy. In the UK, this happens via party politics, in parliament.

There are many sets of interesting ideas and policies that did not make it to full Political Success. Some never got near power; others, more interestingly, managed to get a brief hand on the levers of power but never turned that into a Political Programme. Instead, their grip then slipped: they failed to get a massive positive vote from the electorate. We will meet several of these *Aspirant Political Programmes*, such as Ramsay MacDonald's 1920s Socialism and 'Orange Book' Liberalism, in the narrative section of this book.

In British politics, a Political Programme almost always takes the form of self-reinvention by one of the two major parties. The obvious example, as the brand overhaul was done expressly, was Tony Blair's New Labour. Other reinventions are a bit less overt but can be just as ruthless and just as deep.

Maybe the future will not be two-party, and a totally new UK party will arise and drive its Programme to lasting power. This happened in the first half of the twentieth century, when Labour grew from (almost) nothing to replace the once-mighty Liberals. Right now, however, it seems more likely that if such a new party does appear, it will end up getting osmosed into one of the existing ones – which, of course, will be a huge victory for the newcomer in terms of realizing policy ambitions, although the rosettes of the candidates will be red or blue. Militant Tendency tried to do this to Labour in the 1980s and failed. The Brexit movement tried to do this to the Conservatives in the 2010s and succeeded.

But never say never. Can the Lib Dems fight back? Are the Greens waiting in the wings? Will a new Progressive Alliance come into being?

Models, Values and Stories
A Political Programme has *Models*. These are its 'big pictures' of how the world works: economics, sociology, psychology, geopolitics, technology, (in the future, hopefully) ecology. Religion and a specific theory of history may also form a part.

Different types of picture will weigh more powerfully than others for different Programmes. Thatcherism was not that interested in sociology but driven by economics. The Programme I call '1945 Socialism' was the other way round, with social class at the heart of its thinking.

Programmes that claim to be simply pragmatic and free of any such big-pictures are deceiving us (and themselves, too). No political thought takes place in an intellectual vacuum.

Political Programmes also have *Values*. What is good, and worth protecting and encouraging? What is bad, and needs to be combatted? What behaviour is to be encouraged, and what to be discouraged?

Again, some politicians simply say they are being pragmatic. But they always turn out to have a Value system behind them. Programmes (and people) don't exist in a moral vacuum, either.

Models and values are best taught via *Stories*. Telling and listening to stories is a basic human experience. Ask Hollywood, or any parent. 'Tell me a story!'

Stories confer identity and meaning. Our ancestors lived – and our social emotions evolved – in tribes or clans, to which belonging was nurtured through shared stories from childhood onwards. As they sat at the feet of their elders, maybe round a fire with the infinite, star-filled sky above them, they listened to stories and learnt answers to those huge questions: How does the world work? What sort of people do what sort of things, and what are the consequences? Where do I fit in to all that? What am I supposed to do and why?

Political Programmes tell powerful Stories. There will be two central ones. The *First Story* is about dragon-slaying:

- Something of value…
- …is under threat from a malign force (or forces)!
- How the Programme will come to the rescue.

The *Second Story* is more creative. It's about how good things will happen once the dragon is slain and things are done the way the Programme says they should be.

The First, dragon-slaying Story has a full cast. There are *Villains*, bullying, exploiting, gaming the system, standing in the way of Progress or trying to destroy tradition. If they are also complacent, that's a bonus. There will be *Victims*, decent folk suffering as a result of this villainy. Then along come the *Heroes* (of either gender, of course), charging in to the rescue.

The Story will have its own coded language, so the audience can cheer or boo at the right moments ('Bolsheviks', 'Guilty Men', 'the loony left', 'hard-working families', 'patriots', 'remoaners').

The Second Story is less dramatic but should be the real long-term point of a Political Programme. In it, the Heroes set about building the New Future. These may be the same Heroes as in Story One, but they will be joined by new ones, who will probably be less demonstrative: makers, time-takers, people who insist on thoroughness 'Rome wasn't built in a day,' they will remind us.

Some Political Programmes are more about dragon-slaying. Lloyd George's 1916 Programme was, unsurprisingly, mostly about defeating the German Imperial state on the field of battle. Others put more stress on the Second, future-building Story. Lloyd George's second Programme, after victory, sought to create 'a fit country for Heroes to live in', a forward-looking message (though it still went on about punishing the old, slain, German dragon, in order to appeal to voters, who like a good slaying).

Thatcherism provides an example of a strong mixture of Stories, both pursued with intensity. The trade unions and government bureaucracy were the dragons in the First Story. Entrepreneurs and 'wealth-creators' were the future-creating Heroes of the Second.

Outside democracies, revolutions often have a brilliant First Story but a terrible Second one. Tragically, the First is often used to maintain support for the Second. The Czarist regime in Russia probably had to be overthrown: it was corrupt, outdated, cruel and inept. A monstrous tyranny then replaced it, but the glorious First Story was used to justify that tyranny.

Classical Marxism is all First Story. After the Revolution, a natural, benevolent order is supposed to assert itself automatically. No politics necessary; the state will simply 'wither away'.

A Programme's Models, Values and Stories are its *Worldview*.

Policies
How, exactly, will the dragon be slain? How, precisely, will the New Future be built? The Programme's founders will create an *Action Plan*, a list of *Core Policies,* prioritized in order of urgency. These will be substantial, and many will be radical.

Core Policies must be implemented for a Programme to be meaningful.

A Programme that does a 'U-turn' on a Core Policy has failed. To quote Enoch Powell, a man now rightly unpopular for his views on race but who had a profound understanding of the political process: "It is fatal for any government… to seek to govern in direct opposition to the principles with which they were entrusted with the right to govern."

This does not mean that a Political Programme has *no* room for flexibility. Far from it. As long as it sticks to its Worldview and Core Policies, it can improvise as much as it likes. It can test, tinker with and drop *non-core* policies to meet changing circumstances. Indeed, it must do this. The world never stops changing, and the administration has to come up with responses to these changes. But it cannot ditch its Worldview or Core Policies in the process, otherwise it appears to stand – and arguably does stand – for nothing. Flexibility within an inflexible framework: such is the art of politics.

Various analogies spring to mind. A musician improvising over a chord sequence. A marketer: brands have core values, from which they depart at their peril. But the most helpful analogy is the process of scientific discovery, and I shall look at this in more depth in the next chapter.

The Big New Idea

This is the essence of the Programme. It's what lodges the Programme in people's minds. (Stories lodge the Programme in their hearts, arguably a more important job, but the Big New Idea provides a clear pivotal point around which the Stories must orbit.)

Big New Ideas are infuriatingly simple. They can be just a word or a phrase. Clement Attlee's Socialist Britain was a Big New Idea (Socialism was not a new idea, of course, but Attlee's Programme was about putting it into practice, policy by policy, in a specific time and place). Margaret Thatcher's Enterprise Economy was a Big New Idea. New Labour was a Big New Idea. Brexit was a Big New Idea. People hear the name and know that this is something fresh and that lots of new things will flow from it.

This simplicity is terribly unfair. A Big New Idea is like a great melody. You can think, 'My God, that's beautiful' and at the same time, 'It's just a few notes. Why the hell didn't I think of that? I could be playing 80,000-seater stadia, not doing my usual Saturday night gig at the Dog and Duck!'

In considering Big New Ideas, I find it helpful to add a few sentences to the word or phrase, expanding it a bit to outline core concerns, policies or the general 'feel' of the Programme. So, for example, I adumbrate 'New Liberalism' (the first Big New Idea of the 20th century) by adding, 'The poorest people in the UK are trapped in poverty. We will set up a German-style welfare system to enable them to escape this and lead fulfilling lives. We will pay for it with income and land taxes, not import tariffs, as Free Trade creates wealth.'

This is equivalent to the 'elevator pitch' of a start-up business. In this metaphor, the entrepreneur gets into a lift, and there's one other person in there – the exact person they have been looking to pitch their idea to. This person presses 'six'. The lift begins to move… The entrepreneur has those six floors to convince them. And only six floors. The lift doesn't get stuck. She or he can't hand the target an eighty-page business plan. In a few sentences, what will grab the attention and interest of the target?

Critics of the above object that the world is complex, and add that simplistic solutions can do a lot of damage. It is, of course, true that some Big New Ideas have caused immense damage. Communism and Fascism, for example. But that just shows that there are good and bad Big New Ideas, not that Big New Ideas are bad.

Big New Ideas have to pass the 'elevator' test. End of story. To 'quotejack' EM Forster, 'Yes, Oh dear, yes, Big New Ideas are simple.' Military philosopher Carl von Clausewitz wrote, 'Determination in carrying through a simple idea is the surest way to achieve success.'

In the next chapter, I shall look at the history of science, and show how the same logic applies. Science is driven by Big New Ideas that are conceptually profound, radical and annoyingly (to other people in the field, wrestling with the difficulty of it all) simple. Newtonian mechanics is based on three laws. It took Newton years of study to boil it down to those three laws, but there they are now, starkly uncomplicated but overflowing with implications. Darwin's theory of evolution can be reduced to a handful of concepts: inheritance, mutation, overpopulation, competition and speciation.

Slogans
The Big New Idea is not the same as the Slogan of the winning party. Slogans are superficial attention-grabbers. The more you think about them, the emptier they become. Big New Ideas are the opposite: the more you think about them, the more they resonate. "So then we'd have to…" "And then we could…" I define the Big New Idea of Harold Wilson's 1960s 'White Heat' Programme as 'the modernization of Britain through planning, technology, social liberalization, meritocracy and removal of the old boy network'. Plenty to get stuck into there. His election Slogan from 1964 was 'Let's go with Labour!' Go where? Who knows? There was even a hilariously awful single produced by Labour with that name: find it on YouTube and cringe.

A lot of damage can be caused by confusing Slogans and Big New Ideas. Politicians can mouth Slogans and convince themselves that they have a Big New Idea. When they start trying to put the Slogan into action, they find no guidance, no policies that flow from it and (what would have been even more useful) no policies that it renders unacceptable.

What, exactly, is Novelty?
A new Political Programme is a new way of looking at the world and a new set of responses to what is seen. It isn't just triangulation. It isn't just sticking a smart new label on old policies (a technique known in marketing as 'rebadging'). It isn't just doing the direct opposite to what 'the other lot' did, either. Genuinely new Political Programmes construct the world differently.

As a result, they can be ignored or frowned on to start with. Focus groups won't get them. To start with.

The protagonists in the Programme's First Story will initially be ignored, or at least not taken fully seriously, by the old dominant Programme, which will see itself as essentially concerned with other issues.

When the Programme triumphs, the struggles it outlines will take centre stage. New opportunities will be available, too, to drive the Second Story. There will be new ways of flourishing. There may even be new metrics for what flourishing means. Victory? Empire? Equality? GDP growth? Gross National Happiness?

Yet the new Programme isn't total reinvention. The new Programme will also contain some content *carried forward* from old ones. There will be some carried-forward *Models*. Blairism shared Thatcherism's respect for enterprise and market mechanisms. There will be some carried-forward *Values*. Economic growth has been regarded by all recent Programmes as desirable (as we hurtle towards ecological disaster, this may change). There will be some carried-forward *Policies*, even Core ones. The welfare reforms of 1945 Socialism were continued by its 'One Nation' Conservative successor, and this continuity was an important part of the new Programme's message. Even themes or characters from *Stories* may be carried forward, though Stories themselves tend to be fresh for each Programme. Lloyd George's post-1918 Programme and its successor, Tranquillity, were equally keen to protect the nation from the Villain of Bolshevism.

However, all carried-forward content will be remixed and reframed to fit the new narrative (which is why there was also a profound disconnect between the departing Attlee and the new Churchill governments in 1951 – more on this later). This carrying forward will disappoint the more extreme supporters of the Programme, who will want to reinvent everything, but these hotheads must be overruled.

*Un*democratic Political Programmes can aspire to be all-reinventing and start from Year Zero. In France in 1789, in Russia in 1917, in Germany in 1933, in China in 1949, in Cambodia in 1975, everything was remade. This planned rebuilding will include human nature. Disaster is the inevitable result. Stories can change people's perception of themselves, but not their underlying humanity. The 'Perfect Nazi' or the 'New Soviet Man' was always an illusion.

By contrast, changes of Political Programme in democracies, *Democratic Revolutions,* allow radical change to combine with a measure of continuity and with continuing human messiness and diversity. That's the wonder of democracy. Not that it 'gives the people what they want' (it gives a majority of people what they want), but that it enables a nation's institutions to adapt to a perpetually changing world in line with popular views and without bloodshed.

The Goddess of Fortune

What causes Political Programmes to be successful? Accurate models? Deeply-felt Values? Compelling Stories? Well thought-through Core Policies? A clear, strong Big New Idea? The right balance of innovation and continuity? Or some extra factor, like a brilliant Leader?

I suspect they need all these things, but they also need something else. That extra something is that cruel, unfair thing called luck. Political Programmes get their timing right. They capture a *Zeitgeist*, a deep swell of concern and/or ambition in the general public (or in enough members of that general public to give the Programme legitimacy and power). It is, of course, fiendishly hard to tell in advance what those swells of feeling are going to be. If that were easy, politics would be easy.

As a result, the builders of great Political Programmes are like successful artists or entrepreneurs. They have a passionate, in some ways irrational, belief about what the real issues are and what needs doing, now. They assert that belief, often initially to general derision. They stick to their guns, because that's the kind of person they are. They begin to find themselves attracting like minds. Support for their Big New Idea grows. This support becomes a wave, that builds and builds and finally takes their Programme to glory. Right person, right idea, right time, right place.

The Victorian historian Thomas Carlyle took this idea further, and argued that history was actively propelled by 'Great Men', who ruthlessly drove it in a direction it wasn't otherwise going to go in. I see little evidence of this (and much more evidence of narcissistic individuals proclaiming this is the case and they are examples of it).

The opposite view was expressed by Edwardian politician Arthur Balfour, who commented that the winner of the 1906 Liberal landslide, Henry Campbell-Bannerman, was 'a mere cork, dancing on a torrent which he cannot control'.

The truth seems to lie somewhere between these extremes. Political Programmes ride the Zeitgeist, but they still have to be well crafted, led and executed. The nineteenth-century German chancellor, Bismarck, whom nobody could mistake for a dancing cork, wrote: 'Statesmen do not have to make history, but if they hear the sweep of the mantle of God in events around them, they must jump up and catch the hem.'

Of course, this raises the interesting question of what determines the rise and fall of Zeitgeists. It's a fascinating one – but beyond the scope of this book, in which I have just assumed that this rise and fall takes place. One thing, perhaps, I can say is that the rise and fall is not uniform. The wheel of fortune does not turn at a constant rate. Instead, business author Douglas B Holt compares the process to the concept of 'punctuated equilibrium' in evolutionary science, whereby species evolve quickly, then stay constant, often for a long time, then disappear fast. So, says Holt, do Zeitgeists: meteoric and attention-grabbing to start with, they then enjoy a longish period of dominance, before suffering a sudden collapse into irrelevance as the world changes and people's challenges change with it. Political Programmes, as you will see, rise and fall with them.

I shall argue that there have been ten Political Programmes in British politics since the start of the twentieth century (or eleven if one counts the Programme of the Marquess of Salisbury, who was in power, with a Programme endorsed in 1895, when that century began). The Programmes are:

- New Liberalism
- The two brief Programmes of Lloyd George
- 'Tranquillity' (Inter-war Conservatism)
- 1945 Socialism (which actually began in 1940 – I'll explain later)
- Fifties 'One Nation' Conservatism
- 'White Heat' Modernization
- Thatcherism
- New Labour
- Populist 'Brexit' Nationalism

No, that list doesn't quite fill out the entire period from 1900 to now.

The 1920s saw two brief attempts at government by the then-new Labour Party, but those were both Aspirant Political Programmes that failed to achieve a majority. Socialist government would have to wait a couple of decades.

The National Governments from 1931 to 1940 were essentially a continuation of 'Tranquillity' rule.

The 1970s were a time when both major UK parties attempted to create Political Programmes, but failed (though one of them did manage to enact one of its Core Policies, so was a kind of semi-success, even without a Great Endorsement).

And what about the 2010s? The Coalition never quite made it to Political Programme status – more on this in the history section. What about the second Cameron administration, after his outright election win in 2015? It didn't last long. The May administration? That was a transitional government, trying in vain to stem the rise of the next full-on Political Programme, which already had a hand on the levers of power but wanted (and would get) much more. More on this later, too.

I have not included Scottish or Welsh Nationalism on my list, though the rise of these Big Ideas in their home nations would be a fascinating topic. Readers in those nations have a right to object, but I am more familiar with the history of Westminster politics.

I have restricted this model-building to the UK, too. My guess is that it can usefully be extended to other nations. The USA has seen some classic Political Programmes: Theodore Roosevelt's 'Square Deal', FDR's 'New Deal', Lyndon Johnson's 'Great Society'. And even in countries more used to coalitions, Big New Ideas rise and fall, and small thought-groups and powerful Leaders usually drive them, initially against a wall of opposition.

A Political Programme is…

"A Politically Successful set of Models, Values, Stories and Core Policies, grouped around a Big New Idea."

<u>Politically Successful</u>
    It catches and rides a wave of popular opinion
    It gains power and holds it for a substantial period of time

<u>Models</u>
    The 'big picture'
    How the world works: tech, economics, sociology (etc.)

<u>Values</u>
    Good vs Bad, Right vs Wrong

<u>The Central Stories</u>
    The First (Slaying the Dragon)
- Something of value…
- …under threat from a malign force
- The Rescue. How the good guys will win.

    The Second (Building the New Future)
- The good things that will happen once virtue prevails.

The Models, Values and Central Stories add up to a <u>Worldview</u>

<u>Core Policies</u>
    Radical and substantial
    Prioritized
    'Not for turning'

<u>The Big Idea</u>
    A distillation of all the above into a word, phrase or sentence.
    "What the Programme is all about."
    Much more than a Slogan

<u>'New'</u>
    Genuinely original thinking…
    …though some old material will be carried forward and remixed

The Model behind the Model

I'd like to talk a little about the inspiration for my model. This might seem self-indulgent, but I ask you to bear with me, as this will not only make the model's workings clearer but also root it in a supremely powerful existing process.

My model of how politics works is based on a model of how science works. This model of science was expressed in two classic texts. The first was Thomas S Kuhn's book *The Structure of Scientific Revolutions*. The second was a reply to that, an essay by philosopher Imre Lakatos called *The Methodology of Scientific Research Programmes*.

Kuhn's book, published in 1962, is best known for having coined the word 'Paradigm', which is now often used for any collection of ideas and has become debased. "We need a new paradigm!" exclaims an eager marketing executive, whereupon everyone else in the meeting starts staring out of the window or wondering when the coffee will be brought in.

Lakatos, writing a few years later, employed a term which has stayed fresher. Rather than 'Paradigms', he talked about 'Research Programmes'. There are subtle differences between the two concepts which I shall touch on later, but they tell the same essential story.

To get a deeper understanding of what these terms mean, it's best to look at the context in which they arose. Kuhn wrote his book in response to an argument in the philosophy of science about the question, 'How does science progress?'

In the nineteenth century, it was generally believed that science progressed by discovering more and more laws. It just got better and better. (Victorian historians like GB Macaulay thought the same about history.) It did this by observing phenomena, hypothesizing laws from these observations, testing these laws by experiment and proving the laws if the experiments worked.

The twentieth-century philosopher Karl Popper disagreed. Annoyed by a rising tide of what he called 'pseudo-scientific' ideas, including psychoanalysis and Marxism, he argued that real science progressed by observing phenomena, hypothesizing laws from these observations, testing these laws by experiment and *dis*proving them if the experiments *didn't* work. He went as far as to say that scientific 'knowledge' wasn't really knowledge at all but a series of 'conjectures' that hadn't yet been refuted.

Popper contrasted this acceptance of fallibility on the part of proper scientists with the behaviour of pseudo-scientists, who, when their theories failed by making predictions that turned out wrong, devoted their time and energy to finding ever more ingenious ways of explaining the failure away, defending their precious theories against inconvenient reality (and often launching *ad hominem* attacks on opponents, as 'bourgeois' or 'repressed').

This appeared to be a major step forward, as it cleared up the rules of the game. Then Kuhn came along and spoilt things by pointing out that actual science didn't work the way Popper suggested, and could never do so. In actual science, Kuhn said, big overarching 'core' theories, such as Newtonian mechanics or Darwin's theory of evolution, are <u>not</u> open to disproof. They are *assumed*, with the same level of unquestioning acceptance shown by Marxists and Freudians.

When anomalies emerge, scientists do not ditch Newton or Darwin, but do exactly the same as Popper's pseudo-scientists; they look for ways of squaring the anomaly with their overarching theory. They can do this in various ways:

- by creating new sub-theories
- by patching up existing sub-theories
- by making specific criticisms of whatever experiment or observation(s) had produced the anomaly
- by simply ignoring the anomaly.

The last of these might seem terribly unscientific, but was not uncommon. For years, astronomers had known that the planet Mercury appeared to move in a way that didn't fit the Newtonian model, but this had not led to any rewriting of the big theory, only to intrigued puzzlement. One day, Newtonians were sure, an explanation would be found. In fact, the observations only came to make sense once Einstein had produced his Newton-transcending Theory of Relativity.

'Paradigm' was Kuhn's word for the big intellectual tent where these overarching theories are assumed and where practical, day-to-day scientific work is carried on in the light of them. He called the work that is done within this tent *Normal Science*, as it is what scientists normally do: measuring things, creating and testing new concepts and/or sub-theories, inventing or refining technologies. Normal Science, he argued, uses Popperian trial and error about its sub-theories and technologies, being prepared to drop them if they don't work. But while this is going on, the core beliefs at the heart of the Paradigm remain beyond question.

That point was well taken, but it raised a new issue. If the big theories are beyond question, how does science progress? Is it just a shouting match between two groups of equally convinced fanatics? The 'geocentric' model of the universe where all heavenly bodies revolved round the earth reigned supreme in the classical world and Europe's Middle Ages, but was eventually ditched. How? Why?

Kuhn, arguably more a historian than a full-on philosopher, was unclear about this, but Lakatos took things further by producing a logical model of Research Programme (= Paradigm) change.

According to Lakatos, anomalies in a Research Programme begin to build up over time. More and more things happen in ways the big theory says they shouldn't. After a bit of work, these get explained, but the explanations become more and more convoluted and less and less useful. Rather than make interesting new predictions, the new explanations just account for the anomaly (plus a few cases like it). The new explanations are simply patching the big theory up. Over time, the Programme becomes full of such patches, like an old bicycle tyre. Lakatos called models in that condition 'Degenerating Research Programmes' (and argued that Marxism and Freudianism fell into this category).

So what causes change? Lakatos said that the Degenerating Research Programme keeps chugging along, however convoluted and clogged with patches it has become, and will not be rejected *until a better big, overarching model appears.*

'Better', for Lakatos, meant a number of things. First, the new overarching model explains the biggest anomalies that have started to bug the old one (or most of these anomalies, anyway). Secondly, it also explains all (or most of) the phenomena that the old model had, once so proudly, explained. Thirdly, it comes armed with new concepts, so offers exciting new avenues for both pure research and technological development. Fourthly, it will stick its neck out make bold predictions – which then come true. Fifthly, it has an aesthetic appeal: it is simpler.

Lakatos was keen to point out that the new, better Research Programme doesn't appear fully-fledged. It takes time to develop, 'slowly, by a long, preliminary process of trial and error.' Darwin took twenty-five years to finesse his theory of evolution before he went public with it in 1859, and the Programme didn't really get its stranglehold on biological thinking till the rediscovery of the work of Gregor Mendel on heredity in 1900. (Interestingly, 1859 saw the publication of another, similar but less worked-through theory of evolution, that of Alfred Russell Wallace, while in 1900, three researchers in three different countries independently rediscovered Mendel. There is a Zeitgeist in science, as well as politics.)

During its development period, the developing Research Programme faces powerful challenges that could overwhelm it. To start with, there will be things that the new model doesn't explain well. Then once it is public, supporters of the old one will fight back. "Am I descended from a monkey through my grandmother or my grandfather?" Bishop Samuel Wilberforce asked Darwinist TH Huxley. More seriously, physicist Lord Kelvin doubted that, given the age of the earth, evolution would have had enough time to come up with humanity. (Darwin was genuinely troubled by this, but the earth has turned out to be much older than Kelvin thought.)

The new Programme simply gets its head down and keeps gathering evidence, dealing with problems and developing sub-theories. At the same time, the old one becomes more and more clogged up. Ultimately the new one begins to accelerate past the old.

A key moment in this overtaking is a Crucial Experiment. A situation is imagined, where one theory predicts one outcome and the rival theory predicts a different one. This situation is then created in a lab (or sought out: astronomers have travelled the world to make crucial observations). The result decides between the two Programmes. This practice goes right back to Newton's time. The term, or its Hogwarts-like Latin version, *experimentum crucis*, was first used by Newton's near-contemporary Robert Hooke. An even earlier philosopher of science, Francis Bacon, talked about a 'crucial instance'.

Success in such an experiment can create what writer Malcolm Gladwell calls a tipping point. After failing one of these, the old theory, which up to that point was putting up a strong rearguard action, will go into rapid and irreversible decline. Galileo's observations of moons orbiting the planet Jupiter are often regarded as the Crucial Experiment that tipped the scales against geocentric astronomy.

Kuhn believed that the new Paradigm used a different language to the old one, and that, as a result, practitioners within the old and the new ones lived in different, irreconcilable conceptual worlds. Lakatos disagreed: people in different Research Programmes can and do talk to one another about sub-theories and technology. He pointed out that no new Programme sweeps away the entire edifice of the old one. He talked instead of new Programmes being 'grafted' onto old ones, the way that in horticulture one plant is inserted into the base of another and then grows from it. Much technology and some sub-theories get carried forward. We no longer accept Newtonian mechanics to be *the* explanation of the cosmos or the workings of the sub-atomic world, but we still build skyscrapers and bridges on principles based on it.

Both Kuhn and Lakatos agreed that the dethronement of a Paradigm/Research Programme does not amount to a complete, watertight logical disproof of it. Even a Crucial Experiment can be argued round if you are clever enough. In terms of pure logic, you can still believe the sun goes round the earth – but don't expect to make a lot of progress intellectually or get much respect from the scientific community. It's like trying to drive from London to Edinburgh in a Model T Ford: give it a go, but don't be upset if almost every other vehicle on the road overtakes you or you end up on the hard shoulder of the Doncaster bypass with steam coming out of the bonnet.

And what about politics?
This book argues that the history and practice of politics is very similar to this.

Political Programmes work with a tightly-knit core of Models, Values, Stories and Core Policies, which they do not and cannot deviate from. These are the equivalent of science's big, unquestioned Paradigms/Research Programmes: Newtonian mechanics, Darwinian evolution.

While holding fiercely to this core, Political Programmes can and do come up with lesser policy ideas in response to events. These can be reversed and often are – just as sub-theories or technologies in Normal Science come and go. I'll call them 'Normal Politics'.

Programme change takes place in a similar way to the Kuhn/Lakatos model of science, too. Over time, the Models, Values, Stories and Core Policies that speak so clearly to one cohort of voters begin to lose their resonance. Either the much-trumpeted core policies don't work, or stop working, or turn out to have damaging, previously unexpected consequences. They may be reversed (the classic 'U-turn'). The

Programme becomes a Degenerating one, no longer aspiring to lead events but struggling to keep up with them.

However, Degenerating scientific Research Programmes like geocentric astronomy can lumber along, and will do so until something better comes along. The same is true in politics. Attacking a failing Political Programme can be good for team morale and can chip away at voter support – but the way to win back serious, lasting power is to come up with something radically different and clearly better: a new Political Programme, with new Models, Values, Stories and Core Policies.

Like a great scientific theory, this will (usually) have been worked on, long and hard. In science, this is often done by one great mind (though Newton described himself as having 'stood on the shoulders of giants'). In politics, the intellectual heft is more usually provided by a group of people. (Modern science is, I suspect, more of a team game, too.)

The new Political Programme, though radical, does not have to reinvent everything. In science, many concepts, sub-theories and technologies are 'grafted' from one Research Programme to another. Similarly, new Political Programmes will carry forward some ideas and policies from previous incumbents.

In science, there may be an interregnum period when two theories are battling for supremacy. The analogy to this in politics is the time after a new Political Programme first gets its hands on the levers of power – a grasp that can still be highly provisional (as the history in the second part of this book will show), before the new Programme truly cements its grip (or, of course, fails to). In science, a Crucial Experiment accelerates this process. The equivalent in politics is clearer and more brutal, a substantial majority in a general election.

The old Programme, like the old theory, is defeated at that point. However, in politics as in science, some diehards will cling to old models, years after they've been ditched by everyone else. The train has moved on, but not everyone will be on board.

Kuhn called the change of one Paradigm (Research Programme) to another, a Scientific Revolution. In democratic politics, one can talk of Democratic Revolutions.

I must end this section by admitting that the analogy is not perfect. No analogy is. Science is a search for absolute, eternal truth. Politics is less ambitious: the search for the best solutions for current and looming problems. Science has a static target, politics a moving one.

As a result of this, scientific Research Programmes last much longer than Political Programmes. Darwinism is still going strong; by contrast, the life-cycle of a democratic UK Political Programme is only about fifteen years. Sometimes less. Maybe at some time in the future, a Political Programme will come into being that will have greater longevity – but given the pace of change in the world, this seems unlikely. With the human capacity for corruption, smugness and gaming systems, that seems a good thing. Fifteen(or so)-year political cycles are good for us.

However, despite these differences, I consider that the nature and life-cycles of big scientific theories and of Political Programmes are amazingly similar. Both science and democracy have been successful due to their mixture of trial-and-error (in Normal Science and Normal Politics), the clarity given by a powerful overarching vision, and the flexibility to allow, over time, change at the profoundest level.

Research Programmes and Scientific Revolutions

Thomas Kuhn, The Structure of Scientific Revolutions
Imre Lakatos, The Methodology of Scientific Research Programmes

Research Programmes (Paradigms)
    Based on a big, overarching core theory (e.g., Newton, Darwin)…
        …which is *not* questioned, but assumed
    'Normal Science' is carried on within the Programme:
        Building models of the world based on the big theory
        Creating technologies to solve real-world problems
        Ditching or amending stuff that doesn't work

The Programme starts to Degenerate
    Anomalies in the core theory start building up
    These are either ignored, or explained away by:
        New or amended sub-theories
        Criticism of the experiment that produced the anomaly
    But these explanations become 'patches'
        Ever more convoluted
        Making increasingly less-interesting predictions

Programmes are only changed when something better comes along, that:
    Explains the anomalies
    Fits (most of) the existing technological knowledge
    Offers new areas of research and technology opportunities
    Makes bold predictions, which then come true
    Is simpler

A Scientific Revolution takes place
    Not instantly: the old model still has supporters (and always will)
    A Crucial Experiment convinces a critical mass of scientists
    Some sub-theories and technologies are carried forward into the new model.

Politics follows a very similar pattern.

Rise and Fall:
The Life-Cycle of a Political Programme

Lakatos set out a formal life-cycle for scientific Research Programmes. I shall do this for Political Programmes.

Genesis

No two Political Programmes form in exactly the same way. Yet there are usually common processes and types of individual involved.

Many aspects of the Worldview and Core Policies will have already been laid out in a *Canon*, which contains a small number of *Sacred Texts*. An example of the latter: Margaret Thatcher once interrupted a speech from a well-meaning centrist Tory by producing a copy of FA von Hayek's *The Constitution of Liberty* from her bag and thumping it down on the table in front of her. "This is what we believe!" she exclaimed.

Hayek's book was over a decade old by then. However, part of a Programme's Canon can be written as the Programme evolves. The Beveridge Report, a Sacred Text of 1945 Socialism was written when the Programme already had one hand firmly on the tiller of national power (that was in 1942. I'll explain the dates later). LT Hobhouse's *Liberalism* was published five years into the New Liberal Programme. The most important such texts prove popular with the commentariat, but best of all with the public at large. Beveridge sold 600,000 copies.

Outside democratic politics, two classic examples of Sacred Texts are *Mein Kampf* and Chairman Mao's *Little Red Book*.

In practical terms, a Political Programme often begins its long journey to power when a number of *Founders* meet and develop the intellectual core. I call this the *Crucible Group*. They may not assemble with such a grand intention; they may simply like each other then discover a shared passion, vision, intensity and love of the same Sacred Texts. A sense of urgency soon focuses their bright, multi-faceted lights – every member of a Crucible Group brings something different to the party – into a laser beam, as they debate and assemble the key Models, Values, Stories and Policies.

This focusing can take a while – and must: it has to be got right. But slowly (and argumentatively) the Programme's essence comes together. What Models and Values do they share most deeply? What are the Central Stories? What are the most pressing issues? What are the policy options to solve them? How, exactly, would these policies be implemented? In what order? Check: are there alternatives? Can we learn from the experience of other countries? Core Policies must be thought through with particular care, as the Programme will ultimately stand or fall by them.

As the group does this work, the Big New Idea becomes clearer – what the Programme is really all about. This, in turn, drives further development of the Programme. A virtuous circle comes into being, of clarification, exploration of possibilities, understanding linkages and, above all, perhaps, a growing sense of energy and possibility. "This will be big!"

There may be more than one such group, but to keep things simple, I shall try and associate one principal formative group with each Programme. Certainly, if your ambition is to create a new Political Programme, you should form a Crucible Group. Get the very best minds you can to join it and understand what its jobs are: to clarify and agree on the core set of Models, Values, Stories and Policies and to distil their essence, the Big New Idea. Accept that this may take a while, and worry away relentlessly at what you truly believe and what you must do.

If the Crucible Group is purely composed of intellectuals, a second group may be necessary once the Crucible Group has done its job. This is an *Action Group*, whose job it is to get out there and promote the new ideas. It will probably contain the leading thinkers, but also needs:

- A marketing/media expert. Dominic Cummings' understanding of new media was essential to the success of the 2016 Brexit campaign. Cummings was duly feted by the Conservatives, but later ditched: being in the Crucible or Action Group doesn't mean a place at the top table, where, in the end, non-party mavericks don't fit.
- Doers, organizers, people who 'make things happen'.
- A backer, someone with deep pockets who can fund research, publicity etc.

Some Crucible Groups may morph into Action Groups. But they don't always.

Though egalitarians like to think this isn't true, a Political Programme needs a *Leader*. The Leader is the driving force of the Programme, which may well end up being named after them: people talk about 'the Macmillan years', Thatcherism, Blairism.

The Leader is usually part of the Crucible and/or Action Groups, but this is not always the case. Leaders can join a Programme when it is underway. This may sound odd, but it may happen if a group of Founders have successfully captured the Zeitgeist but there is no figure among them with sufficient potential to become a lasting, successful PM. The Programmes of both 1906 and 1924 started off with leaders (Campbell-Bannerman, Bonar Law) who were able, but soon had to resign due to ill health, allowing names who became more famous (Asquith, Baldwin) to take – and keep – the reins. Harold Macmillan was the third 'One Nation' Conservative PM. His predecessors had been Winston Churchill, who was too old by the time the Programme came to power, and Anthony Eden, who had health issues and probably wasn't PM material anyway. After them, Macmillan took command of the Programme and steered it for seven years. Boris Johnson took over from Nigel Farage as Leader of Populist 'Brexit' Nationalism from the moment he decided to campaign for Leave, in February 2016. Farage had no parliamentary presence and was too much of a loose cannon. (Current Brexiter critics of Johnson argue that he, too, is flawed, and the real Leader of their Programme is yet to emerge.)

These 'mid-flight joiner' Leaders aren't just jumpers on a bandwagon. They will have been involved in the Programme for a long time. Their loyalty runs deep. Macmillan wrote a core text in 1938 for the Programme he came to lead in 1957. Johnson, despite his apparent hesitation in supporting Brexit in early 2016, had years of journalistic experience of mocking the EU.

Leaders who led Political Programmes from the start include Clement Attlee, Harold Wilson, Margaret Thatcher and Tony Blair.

All Leaders' depth of commitment to the Programme will be tested over time. But they will not falter, however much events or ambitious individuals try and force policy in other directions. I've already compared them to artists and entrepreneurs. Artists have a personal vision and dedicate themselves to expressing it, whatever the consequences. Entrepreneurs do the same: when the enterprise grows, 'keeping the flame' is arguably their most important job. If they are savvy, they will have delegated sales, marketing, finance, research, delivery and other functions to experts in these fields. The entrepreneur chooses and marshals the top people, makes the big strategic decisions and perpetually reminds all stakeholders (employees, customers, suppliers etc.) what the company is really 'about'. They set and maintain the tone. Leaders of Political Programmes do exactly the same.

To achieve this, Leaders must be charismatic and be great communicators. Clement Attlee was an exception here. He was not charismatic, and didn't want to be. But that was in a pre-television era. He was, however, greatly loved within the Labour movement, where people spoke affectionately of 'our Clem'.

They must master media, especially new, rising ones. Stanley Baldwin was famous for his reassuring chats over the exciting new medium of his era, radio. Macmillan, who straddled the pre- and post-television eras, acquired the relevant skills once in office, mastering TV in time for the 1959 election. Harold Wilson, who followed him, was a natural for the medium. In the modern USA, we have seen Donald Trump taking to Twitter.

Leaders need a strong work ethic and to be good team-managers. Johnson seems to be the exception here, missing a number of key COBRA meetings at the start of the Covid pandemic and, rather than creating a team of heavyweights, surrounding himself with loyalists (there are reasons why he had to do the latter: I'll explain later).

Leaders also need to be deep thinkers (or need*ed* to be, anyway). Asquith abandoned a very successful legal career for politics. Attlee and Macmillan both wrote serious political books. Wilson didn't, but was regarded as one of the cleverest men in Whitehall. Thatcher was part of a passionately intellectual Crucible Group. However, more recent Programme Leaders have come more from the Sales or PR Departments than R and D. This may or may not be a trend.

Leaders often have a *Foil*, someone with a specific skill in an area the Leader lacks and whom the Leader can rely on for support and balance. This is often true with entrepreneurs, too, though in business the Foil is usually content to remain out of the limelight. Few politicians are this bashful. Examples? Asquith and Lloyd George. Wilson and Roy

---

Political Programme Leaders

Long history of involvement with the Programme
    (but don't have to have led from the start)
Like artists or entrepreneurs, they
    Do not waver
    Choose and marshal the top people
    Make big strategic decisions
    'Keep the flame': set and maintain the tone
Must be good communicators
    Master the media of their era
Strong work ethic
(Usually) Deep thinkers
May have a Foil
Are lucky!

Jenkins. Thatcher and (a rare example of a Foil who was happy in the background) Whitelaw. Blair and Brown. Later, the Foil may turn against the Leader, as happened in the first and last of the above examples.

Finally, as I've said, Leaders need to be lucky. The changing Zeitgeist happens to suit them. Leaders may lead people, but they do so from atop the crest of a wave.

Catching On

Right now, however, the new Political Programme is still an *Aspirant*. It does not have power yet, just hopes that it will and is making grand plans in the light of that hope.

It is beginning to attract supporters – the first sign that it has what it takes. People are energized by it. "Yes! At last! This is about me!" The most passionate of these will become *fans*, as loyal to the cause as football season-ticket holders or those people who queued outside bookshops for the midnight release of the next Harry Potter.

This enthusiasm is necessary. At the start of things, signing up to the new Programme can be an act of courage. The Aspirant Programme will be unpopular – amid the ranks of the people that will end up supporting it, let alone with the rest of the world. The first Thatcherites were looked on as cranks within the early 1970s Conservative Party. One member of the Programme's Crucible Group, Keith Joseph, was nicknamed 'the mad monk'. In 2013, a leading Tory – we never found out who – described Brexiters as 'mad, swivel-eyed loons'.

However, the new Programme will have a powerful ally within its 'natural' home party: frustration. The genesis of a new Programme will usually happen at a time when a party has been out of office for a while (not always; the most recent change of Political Programme was a Palace Revolution – more on this later – within the Conservative Party). There will be a sense of anger at that idleness. Once the new Programme is seen as offering a real chance of regaining office, people who might have been sceptical to start with will begin grouping round it. Full-on opponents will be sidelined. Harold Wilson told the 1962 Labour Conference: "The long years in the wilderness are nearing their end." To an audience of politicians starved of power for over a decade, that was crack cocaine.

However, the most powerful ally of all is the mysterious power of the Zeitgeist. Aspirants that turn into full-on Political Programmes tap into this, and it propels them to success.

Three Leaps Forward
More fans. Less cynicism from within the party. The tide is rising – but it will not do so at an even pace. Aspects of the Programme will still meet backlashes (now, more from outside the party than from within). Academics will be produced to discredit the Models. Values will be questioned. Policies will be deemed unworkable. (Stories, alone, remain incontrovertible: you either love them or loathe them.) Mostly, these attacks can be ignored. Being ripped to shreds from a position radically different to your own is a mark of distinction. On social media, fans will leap to the Programme's defence.

The Programme's most dangerous enemies are arguably closer to hand. These are potentially powerful allies who say they would support you *if* you watered the Action Plan down in a few ways. These should be resisted – in a friendly manner, of course. Stay firm, but keep talking to them. If a Programme truly has the Zeitgeist on its side, then momentum will soon carry it past the need for such semi-allies. These people will probably join you later, suddenly affected by amnesia about their previous objections.

At the same time, the Programme's thinkers must retain a bit of flexibility this early in its life. A new idea might be suggested that really does fit the Worldview and Action Plan. The world is perpetually changing, too: aspects of the Programme may need to change to match this, especially if there is a long gap between the Crucible Group meetings and the actual achievement of power. Arguably, the Crucible Group for 1945 Socialism formed in 1931, just after the party's massive defeat.

There will be pauses in progress, and maybe even slips backwards, but also sudden giant leaps forward. It's hard to categorize these leaps, but I'm building a model, so I must come up with some typical ones. Three milestones I would like to highlight are:

- when the Leader (or the leader at the time) gains Significant Influence
- when the Programme gets its First Taste of actual Power
- when the Programme gets its Great Endorsement.

In those cases where the Leader is on board from the start, a major step forward for the Programme is when he or she is formally elected to a position of *Significant Influence*. For Attlee, Wilson, Thatcher and Blair, this moment came when they were elected party leader. This is a great moment for the Programme, as parties tend to unite round a new (or newly-respected) Leader. Till then, the Programme has at best been one (albeit growing and vibrant) strand of party opinion. Now, it is The Party Line (no doubt still dogged by dissent, but dissent is now seen as unconstructive: there is power to be won).

Aspirant Political Programmes can get this far, then fail. In these cases, the Programme is popular with party activists but fails to excite the wider voting public. Those of left-wing Labour leaders, such as Michael Foot and Jeremy Corbyn, tend to suffer this fate. The Conservative Party, usually more alert to what voters want, is less prone to this.

The next move is from Significant Influence to actual Power. The Liberals are asked to form a minority government in 1905. The Conservatives win the 1951 election. Labour wins the 1964 election. This might seem to be the crucial change, but it is not. A *First Taste* of power is almost always tenuous.

In a democracy, this can mean being part of a coalition, or in a minority government, or having a tiny majority, or even having a slightly bigger majority but being under a barrage of sustained criticism (the last of these was the case for Thatcherism, whose First Taste of Power came via a majority of 43, but which remained embattled for much of its first term). In undemocratic politics, the revolution is unfinished: Russia's 1917 February Revolution removed the Czar but did not bring the Bolsheviks sole power.

In all cases, democratic or undemocratic, the Programme's opponents still have a lot of clout. They fancy their chances and do their damnedest to kill this upstart. Many people still write the new Programme off as a 'flash in the pan'. Its grasp on power, they think, is probationary and will soon slip.

Sometimes they are right. The electorate can take the Aspirant Programme for a test drive but end up handing the keys back to the salesperson. Classic examples are the 1929 Ramsay Macdonald administration, Ted Heath's 1970/4 administration and the Liberal

Democrats' 'Orange Book' movement. In all these cases, the Programme had one hand on the lever of power, a working but small majority in the first two examples, membership of a coalition in the third. Rather than stick to their Core Policies and go on to greater things, all of them then made U-turns. Macdonald cut unemployment benefit. Heath did a series of U-turns. The Lib Dems raised student fees. All these actions can be rationally explained as logical reactions to events, but in all cases the electorate was unforgiving. Rightly so, in my view. As the old adage has it: 'If you don't stand for something, you'll fall for anything.'

What a true Political Programme needs instead, and gets next, is a full-on roar of general approval, a *Great Endorsement*. The Great Endorsement is the 'Political Success' in my definition of what a Political Programme is. That is what separates it from an Aspirant one, which ends up just a clever set of ideas or an interesting (to the political historian) movement.

In democratic politics, this means *a substantial election victory*. The Liberals in 1906, Lloyd George in 1918, the Conservatives in 1924, Labour in 1945, the Conservatives in 1955, Labour in 1966, the Conservatives in 1983, Labour in 1997 (an unusual Great Endorsement, as it leapfrogged any tentative First Taste of Power and catapulted straight to full power), the Conservatives in 2019.

How substantial? If asked to pin down a precise figure, I would say 60 seats or more. 100 is the ideal: there's something special about the 'ton', like a century in cricket. However, (to keep the cricket analogy going) 60 in a low-scoring game can be a match-winning innings. In practice, election results tend to be either close or convincing, with little ground in between. But there *are* 'in between' cases. Margaret Thatcher's 43-

seat majority in 1979 was nice (for her), but many people still thought her position precarious. They didn't think this after her 144-seat win in 1983. Ted Heath's 30-seat win in 1970 was insufficient: he was unable to enact one half of his Core Policies and crashed out of office at the next election.

Looking further back in the past, Conservative Andrew Bonar Law won a 74-seat majority in 1922, taking power from the Liberals. However, various factors soon undermined that majority (including his resignation, due to ill health). The new leader, Stanley Baldwin, was forced to go to the country again the very next year – and lost. However, a year later, a third election occurred, and this time Baldwin won by a thumping 210 seats. This was a Great Endorsement for him, which enabled his Programme to run for a full term and then, in the guise of a National Government, to run the country, with a short intermission 1929 – 31, until 1940.

Only with a Great Endorsement does a Programme have the space and time to truly implement its Core Policies. Jim Prior's view that the best governments have small majorities, thus keeping a 'balance of power', is 100% wrong. It is only when given Great Endorsements that administrations can really bring about the deep and difficult changes that they – and the large number of citizens who voted for them – regard as necessary to keep the nation's institutions up to speed with a fast-changing world.

The phrase 'the Will of the People' comes into its own at this moment. Small wins are more a sign that the People aren't really sure, but after a Great Endorsement, there is certainty. The 2016 Brexit referendum, with its relatively close result, was arguably not an expression of such a clear-cut will. The 80-seat win by the Brexit-supporting Conservatives in December 2019 was.

In undemocratic politics, the Great Endorsement is not so much a roar of public approval as the completed seizure of the instruments of government (after which, roars of public approval can be orchestrated). In the Russian example, this is probably the October revolution, though one could argue that the Soviets only had total power with the fall of Vladivostok in October 1922. In Germany, Hitler won the March 1933 election but did not gain an overall majority. He then quickly tightened his grip on power: in August of that year Germany was declared a one-party state.

Pomp
Now the Programme has its hands on the levers of power, firmly and (at least for five, or probably ten, years) immovably. It enters the phase of its *Pomp*.

Time to fully realize its Action Plan. This is the time of *Big Wins*, of radical and long-lasting changes. Lloyd George's 'People's Budget'. The National Insurance and NHS Acts of 1946. Thatcherism's privatization programme. The current Programme's hard Brexit.

Sometimes, these wins will be gained in the teeth of entrenched institutions which were regarded as unassailable by previous Programmes. These institutions have a strong sense of entitlement, and don't give up without a fight. Cue the Programme's *Big Battles*. Asquith and Lloyd George versus the House of Lords. Nye Bevan versus the British Medical Association. Margaret Thatcher versus the trade unions (especially the National Union of Mineworkers). But the Great Endorsement means that these bitter, existential battles can be fought and won. That is exactly what a Great Endorsement is for.

The Action Plan may be pushed further than intended, extending the boundaries of the Big New Idea. The Thatcher era privatization plan initially did not include water companies, which were later privatized.

Why not? The Programme and its Worldview have a crushing majority. The opposition benches will naturally be much thinner, but the government ones will not only be more crowded but filled with new faces: daughters and sons of the new Programme, with an unquestioning loyalty to it, a sense of destiny and a suspicion of whatever went before. The front bench will look different too. Wise Programme Leaders keep a few old, big-hitting rivals in (limited) power, to head off factionalism and because these individuals have genuine ability. But there will be long-serving Programme loyalists who have paid their dues, having been regarded for many years with suspicion by the party's old guard before the Programme's First Taste, and who now expect cabinet posts. It will be payback time.

An unattractive *Triumphalism* can emerge at this time, an unnecessary, hubristic 'rubbing the old enemy's face in it'. "We are the masters now," said 1945 Socialist Hartley Shawcross in 1946. Little was done to support mining communities after crushing of the 1984/5 strike. The current government initially refused to grant full diplomatic status to the EU ambassador in London. Out will come the negative catchphrases, spoken with suitably playground contempt. 1945 Socialists heaped scorn on 'appeasers'. Wilsonite modernizers derided 'grouse-moor' aristocrats. Brexiters taunt 'remoaners'.

This will seem unworthy to objective observers – but remember that people at the heart of a successful Programme will have been fighting against the odds for years. A touch of 'rubbing it in' is only human. However, if a newly-endorsed Programme can rise above this and show magnanimity, that will be for the best, both for the nation and for the long-term reputation of the Programme (the current administration has sensibly backtracked on the EU ambassador's status).

Around the time of its Great Endorsement, the new Programme can enjoy an extra-special moment of triumph, a *Crowning Glory*. This is a great public event which seems to cement in everybody's hearts just how brilliant the Programme is – how much it was needed; how fabulously it has swept away all the old rubbish that was holding the country back. For Fifties 'One Nation' Conservatism, this was Coronation Day in 1953, when the radiant young queen drove past cheering crowds (it was Britain, so she did so through pouring rain) and it was announced *on the same day* that a British expedition had climbed Mount Everest. For Harold Wilson and Roy Jenkins' Programme of modernization, it was England's World Cup victory in 1966. Fate seems to be shouting a great big 'Yes!' to the Programme.

I say, 'around the time', as the Crowning Glory may happen shortly *before* the Great Endorsement. Remember that Political Programmes ride the Zeitgeist, and ever since the First Taste of Power, the tide of that Zeitgeist has been flowing strongly in the Programme's direction (if it is a real Programme, not just an Aspirant), so the exact timing isn't important. The Coronation/Everest was half way between Fifties Conservatism's First Taste and its Great Endorsement, but it was still a great big 'Yes!' for the Programme and its Worldview.

Attempts to manufacture Crowning Glories fail. The 1951 Festival of Britain was supposed to celebrate Attlee's Britain, but by the time it started, the Labour government was staggering towards electoral defeat. The Millennium Experience was supposed to be a Crowning Glory for Blairism, but ended up an embarrassment. Crowning Glories are spontaneous and magical, not the result of planning. That's precisely what makes them special.

As well as these one-off moments, there should be a wider *Cultural Endorsement*, an efflorescence of culture reflecting the Worldview of the new Programme. Great Political Programmes capture a Zeitgeist, and this spirit will also be expressing itself through the arts, both elite and popular. People feel freed and energized. "At last!"

As Political Programmes ride waves, some of this culture will have been around before the Great Endorsement. Georgian poets were writing before Stanley Baldwin's 1924 landslide. The Beatles had smash hits before Harold Wilson's first electoral win, let alone his second. As a Programme hits its stride, it will find a vibrant, deeply-felt culture marching alongside it, that was out of place under the old order but that resonates perfectly with the new order (and that blooms under it). Leaders, in particular, belong. Baldwin was a gentleman; he didn't have to pretend to be. Margaret Thatcher aspired. Tony Blair was young, metropolitan, internationalist.

Cultural Endorsements aren't usually party political. A few artists will come out in formal support for the new Programme – often rather ineptly: Kenny Everett's advice in 1983 to Young Conservatives to 'bomb Russia' probably didn't do Thatcherism or his own image any good. Others may be jollied along to events at Number Ten, where they are photographed next to politicians who are trying to appear casual and everyone looks rather sheepish. Culture and politics may march side by side, but not in lockstep.

Totalitarian Political Programmes will pretend to have such Endorsements, churning out formulaic ones. In democracies (and especially in Britain) we are deeply suspicious of anything that looks forced. Like the Crowning Glory, the independence of the Cultural Endorsement makes it all the more welcome to the Programme, as an affirmation that it is in tune with a powerful, rising national mood.

Usually, culture will also be inspired that is a *Counterblast* to the Programme. The 1930s seethed with writers wanting to disturb 'Tranquillity'. Evelyn Waugh's novels from *Brideshead Revisited* onwards were pot-shots at 1945 Socialism. The response from the Programme to Counterblasts is usually disdain. Harold Macmillan deserves credit for, instead, facing the music and going to a performance of the satirical Counterblast revue *Beyond the Fringe* in 1961. The current Programme has taken a third route, actively demonizing the Counterblast and launching a Culture War.

Counterblasts may be energetic and powerful, but they are still haunted by the Programme. Hatred of Thatcherism was at the heart of to 1980s Counterblast literature. The culture that underpins a new Programme is less reactive. It has found a new way to experience and celebrate life, to which the old Programme is not so much an enemy as an irrelevance.

Great Escapes

Early in its Pomp, the new administration can get away with major policy errors. That is partly due to that thumping majority, but also due to their attunement to the Zeitgeist. Their opponents may fume and history may judge harshly, but a crucial mass of the public at the time is still so relieved to have an administration that sees things their way – 'unlike the last lot' – that they will forgive and/or find someone else to blame. The party may have to sacrifice a bigshot or two, but the Programme will march on. It is too early for real, soul-destroying failure. I call such unpunished errors *Great Escapes* (cue that music...)

Great Escapes will add to that secretly-held belief among activists that the Programme will last not just for a term or two of parliament but much, much longer. The ideas behind the Programme are, after all, The Truth… This is taken to ludicrous extents by totalitarian regimes. Hitler hoped his Reich would last a thousand years. The slogan 'Long Live the Chinese Communist Party!' (*Zhongguo Gongchandang wansui!*) literally wills it to last ten thousand. But even in democratic Programmes, in their Pomp the most fanatical supporters secretly believe they have cracked politics, just as, when we were teenagers, at least a part of us thought we were immortal.

In reality, the Pomp of a Programme usually lasts about five years. Some are lucky enough to ride the wave for longer; others don't get as much time.

The First Big Failure

The Programme in its Pomp appears to be flowing along, conquering all. It has had Great Escapes. Maybe a few bits of Normal Politics turned out to have unexpectedly negative consequences, but Normal Politics can be reversed. Maybe a head or two had to roll – but there were plenty of eager potential replacements jostling to get on the next rung of the ladder.

But at some point, the Programme will hit its *First Big Failure*. This is an event which wasn't in its playbook, and it does not deal with it at all well. Unlike the time of the Great Escape(s), this time, the public (or a significant chunk of it, anyway) is not impressed. A chilling blast of doubt suddenly blows into the previously sealed chamber of power.

The classic example is the Iraq War of 2003. Tony Blair's New Labour had a long and impressive Pomp, but that ended abruptly with the unpopular war, the dishonesty used to justify it, and the subsequent collapse of the newly 'liberated' country into anarchy. I don't have figures, and I don't think such figures exist, but my guess is that a majority of the people who took to London's streets in February 2003 to protest against the war had voted for Blair in 1997 and 2001. Many, possibly most, would not do so again.

The blast is chilling not fatal, however. The Programme is wounded, but still alive. Its core is undamaged. A First Big Failure may be in foreign policy, which may upset the commentariat but not have much effect on the day-to-day lives of most supporters. Many people still feel the Programme in their hearts. This Failure can be explained away.

The Three Fates
The Programme is starting to Degenerate, however. The ancient Greeks were reminded of their unavoidable mortality by the Three Fates, who spun our lives according to a predestined pattern then cut the thread at the end. Similarly, Political Programmes face three remorseless forces that eventually drag them down.

The first of these is a second but more damaging failure, a real *Body-blow*. Despite their apparent mightiness, Political Programmes are essentially brittle – they have dogmas at their heart that will (and should) shatter rather than bend. As circumstances change, these are put under ever more pressure. At some point, there is a horrible crunch where ever-changing reality slams into the Programme and something snaps.

This time, the damage is substantial and lasting. This failure hits the Programme at its heart. It is not about poor execution or foreign policy this time, but the revelation – to voters at home – of a major flaw in its

Model or Values.

Such failures include the Profumo Affair of 1963, the Heath U-turns in the early 1970s and Britain's crashing out of the ERM in 1992. In all these cases, an essential prop of the Programme was destroyed: trust in the ruling class (Profumo), the administration's belief in its own economic policies (Heath) and the government's reputation for economic competence (the ERM debacle).

The second Fate is more chronic. It's more a nagging pain than a disastrous one-off event. I call this the *Slow Strangler*. This is a problem that comes up again and again (and again and again), but which the Programme seems helpless to solve. The Programme wasn't designed to address issues like it, and doesn't have the tools in its armoury to do so. The problem is conceptual as well as practical: this isn't just a lack of a tool but a complete inability to comprehend that such a tool might exist, let alone actually be used. This inability is built into the Programme's Worldview. That proud boast at the start, that the new Programme had The Answer – Mrs Thatcher's version was "There is no alternative!" – turns into a bleat of helplessness: "But there isn't anything else we can do!"

There are alternatives, of course – but the existing Programme and its adherents can't see them. When a new Programme takes power, it can release the grip of the Slow Strangler with one slash of an Alexandrian sword, as it has different Models, Values, Stories and Core Policies.

The most painful examples of Slow Stranglers? 'Tranquil' Stanley Baldwin's failure to understand Hitler. Rationing, which slowly strangled 1945 Socialism. Austerity, which did the same for New Labour and the Coalition that followed it.

The third Fate is a *Big Split*. Major political parties are uneasy coalitions of groups with very different backgrounds and issues. One of the great achievements of a Political Programme is to unite these usually warring tribes under a single banner – for a while, anyway. Over time, however, these differing loyalties start to tell. The 'New Liberals' of 1906 were ripped apart by the split between Asquith and Lloyd George. In the last days of 1945 Socialism, a large chunk of MPs broke off and supported the policy ideas of Nye Bevan, who had resigned from the government. After the departure of Margaret Thatcher, the Conservative Party split over Europe, her normally mild-mannered successor John Major being driven to refer to his Eurosceptic opponents as 'bastards'.

With a seriously split party, policy decisions become as much about trying to appease the splinter group as about the needs of the country or any remaining commitment to the old Worldview or Core Policies.

Limping Along

The relative destructiveness of each Fate can vary from Programme to Programme. For some, the Body-blow is fatal in itself – Fifties Conservatism didn't last long after the Profumo affair. Others keep limping along, being Slowly Strangled or Split (or both).

Why do some Programmes limp along and others vanish quickly? It is partially due to the Zeitgeist: if that changes, which it can with great speed, then the Programme quickly starts to look irrelevant. But they can still blunder on. In power terms, what makes the difference is the quality of the potential replacement. Remember that in Lakatos' model of science, a Degenerating Research Programme continues until something better becomes available. The same is true in politics. Here, 'better' means a Programme with a new set of Models, Values, Stories and Core Policies, a Big New Idea with solutions to the old one's Slow

Strangler(s), with vitality and, above all, with that magic ingredient of *timeliness*, of resonating with a new Zeitgeist. It does not mean 'morally better' in any objective sense, though it will seem that way to its supporters.

Such an alternative may be on hand: Harold Wilson's White Heat was ready and waiting to elbow out Fifties Conservatism. But often the newcomer isn't strong enough yet, and that is when old Programmes limp along. Few politicians just throw in the towel, and even Degenerating Programmes will still have supporters who can explain away every disaster and difficulty. True Believers will support the Programme to their dying day, as it gave them their view of the world, set them free and made them who they are.

Also, voters can be 'small-c' conservative. Given the choice of a set of familiar, albeit rather egg-stained, faces and a new set whom they don't know that well and who don't seem to have a clear, distinct, inspiring alternative, they will stick with the former – as Labour discovered in 1992. Dressing up old policies and having 'one more heave' is rarely enough. Voters have been criticized for this, but I'm with them. In a fast-changing world, if you can't create something genuinely new, then the adventure of government is not for you.

Degenerating administrations will come up with 'Bright Ideas': catchy-sounding policy initiatives that don't have much to do with the original Programme. Some of these work well, others are ignored, others generate sarcasm. John Major's National Lottery fell into the first category, his Citizen's Charter the second, his Cones Hotline the third.

At some point, the Leader will go. Maybe by this point they have already gone – sometimes replaced by their Foil. The *Replacement Leader* is also a believer in the Programme, possibly with a few tweaks.

Replacement Leaders have genuine ability. Major was a highly intelligent man and, according to people who knew him personally, very witty. His pronouncements since leaving office have been statesmanlike and sensible. Gordon Brown went even better: he was probably responsible for saving the UK's, and maybe even the world's, financial system. Replacement Leaders seem to be nicer people than the Leaders they have replaced, too. More nuanced. Less egotistical. There is usually an uptick of voter pleasure at the departure of the old Leader. That tone of voice or that grin had really begun to grate!

But in the end, the Replacement Leader's 'Political Programme Lite' is not enough. A sense of stagnation sets in. Deeper changes of Worldview and fresher, more radical Core Policies are required.

In non-democratic situations, rather than limp along, Degenerating Political Programmes can respond to their failures by *Clamping Down*, ramping up the rhetoric and the violence. In pure survival terms, this can be a hugely effective strategy. As I write this, the dictatorships in Belarus and Myanmar are applying it with dismal success. In both those countries, the tyrants are protected by major global powers, so the rest of the world is unwilling to intervene.

Clamping Down is a disaster, for any dissenters, of course, but also for the rest of the population, who are being led up a cul-de-sac. The nation can no longer change its institutions to keep up with change in the world out there. The dictatorship becomes ever more outdated. Lobsters, apparently, shed their shells a number of times as they grow. The dictatorship becomes like such a creature that, for some reason, is unable to do this, and instead becomes trapped in the smallness and increasing irrelevance of its Worldview. Anyone who visited East Germany in the 1970s or 1980s, and watched (and heard and smelt) smoky Trabants chugging down polluted streets past half-empty shops, will know what I mean.

Sometimes, however, a dictatorship can reinvent itself, or at least a part of itself. The Communist Party managed to do this in China and Vietnam. Mysterious leadership struggles behind firmly closed doors can produce sudden changes: *Palace Revolutions.* Maybe the best that the people on the streets of Minsk or Yangon can hope for is one of these.

Palace Revolutions can also happen in democracies, especially during wartime, when the ballot box isn't a viable option (more on these in the history section that follows). But they do not seem to be common. The only peacetime Palace Revolution in the period of UK history covered by this book is the recent conversion of the ruling Conservative Party to Populist Brexiter Nationalism between 2016 and 2019. Other Democratic Revolutions have all been caused by one party replacing another.

Journey's End
While the old Programme has been Degenerating, a new one will have been gaining ground. The adherents of the old one will have downplayed the importance of that. All Political Programmes suffer from myopia. While they are rising this doesn't matter – arguably it's an advantage. At that time, focusing on the vision is more important than seeing other points of view. Now, however, this will prove disastrous.

The Aspirant new Programme suddenly starts getting real influence. Its Leader is elected to high office (albeit probably in opposition, still). Soon after, it actually gets its First Taste of real Power. The

Degenerating Programme has its *Dethronement* at that moment (literally, in the case of the House of Romanov): it no longer has a monopoly of executive power.

Old-Programme loyalists, convinced of their right to rule, will keep reminding themselves that the newcomers' victory is partial or was a close-run thing. The old order, they say, will soon be restored… These old loyalists will still launch powerful, confident, often dismissive attacks on the upstarts.

If the new rival is a true Political Programme, it will fight these off. It will march on and finally gain its Great Endorsement at the polls. At that moment, the old Programme loses its last vestige or hope of power. It has met its *Waterloo*. This is comparable to the moment in a Scientific Revolution when a Crucial Experiment comes down in favour of the new Research Programme.

Routed now, the Degenerating Political Programme enters its final phase, of *Dissolution*. Once mighty and all-conquering, it is now traumatized and powerless. Its Heroes may well be the Villains of the new narrative, complete with new, derogatory nicknames. The Great Endorsement that has just taken place means that there will be no sniff of power for the now-defunct Programme's party for at least five years, probably more. The party (which was always bigger than the Programme, however much it got into line during the Programme's Pomp) may start tearing itself apart. "You lot got us into this mess!" cry people who never really liked the Programme anyway but who put up with it because it promised office. Pundits will start asking that dreaded question: "Will the x Party ever hold power again?"

The answer is 'almost undoubtedly'. This is a Time of Ashes for the party, but unlike the old Programme, which is now history, the party should at some time recover – once it changes sufficiently. Political Programmes are mortal, like individuals. The parties that host them are like dynasties; they almost always reinvent themselves, after a suitable period of confusion and opposition. A Phoenix will arise from the Ashes, but right now nobody has a clue how, why, what or when.

As I have said, some aspect(s) of the old Programme's thinking/policy-making will have been carried forward and taken up by the new. Old-Programme diehards will take heart from this, accuse the new administration of plagiarism, and mutter that 'our time will come again'. They are wrong. The world has moved on. The asteroid has landed, and the dinos are doomed.

What can the opposition do during this Time of Ashes? It must face up to its situation: the electorate has cast it into the wilderness, and it won't be coming back any time soon. There is opposition to be carried on – the unglamorous business of scrutinizing the government's actions, of 'speaking truth to power', of pointing out inconsistencies, moral failings and the consequences of unwise policies. There will be parliamentary committees with a role in policy formation. MPs still have the ongoing duties of looking after constituents and, where legitimate, their interests. All this can be done with wit, thoroughness and pride. It is the basic job of a Pomp opposition, and carrying it out diligently is important and honourable.

It can look at party admin. David Willetts' *After the Landslide* shows how the Conservatives did this after the Waterloos of 1906 and 1945.

But above all, the opposition to a Programme in its Pomp must wait. Somewhere in the party's midst, ambitious and originally-minded individuals will be getting angry in a new way. They will start working together to clarify their Models, Values and Stories and to create a new Action Plan (which might seem crazy or disloyal or idealistic to most of their colleagues). If the Pomp opposition leader can encourage them, while not really sharing their vision and even coming to realize that they will, at some time, supplant him or her – that is mastery.

Coda

It is a cliché that the only permanent truth is that of change – social, intellectual, economic, geographic, technological, ecological. Change isn't just incremental but produces amazing, totally unexpected and totally new things. It has been that way since the beginnings of life itself. 600 million years ago, creatures developed sight. 60 years ago, we came up with the Internet.

Political Programmes are the best we can do in response to our ever-changing, ever-innovating world. They give us some time to put new or improved institutions in place to match that change. Maybe they even allow us to direct that change a little (how much? That's for another book!) But even at their most impressive, they are only ever based on partial understanding and are doomed to ever-increasing imperfection. Even at the instant of a Programme's mighty Great Endorsement, time and change are already moving on beyond it.

Towards what? Nobody knows. The philosopher Hegel argued that the trial-and-error process of human attempts to model reality was inching towards absolute truth, slowly squeezing out error. But, actually, the opposite is true: reality keeps changing, and our main job is to try and keep up with it. Political Programmes are best-possible attempts to do so, at given historical moments. Hence my comparison between the most influential politicians and artists or entrepreneurs. In an inevitably uncertain world, the best politics is a truly creative art.

The Life-Cycle of a Political Programme

Genesis
    Sacred Text/Canon
    The Crucible Group
    An Action Group
    The Leader
        May be replaced later if not PM material

Gaining Significant Influence
    Aspirant Programmes can fail here (e.g., Foot, Corbyn)

The First Taste of Power
    Aspirant Programmes can fail here
    U-turn(s) are fatal

The Great Endorsement
    A substantial parliamentary majority

Pomp
    Crowning Glory
        (may precede the Great Endorsement)
    Cultural Endorsement and Counterblasts
    Big Battles
    Big Wins
    Great Escapes
    Triumphalism

<u>The First Big Failure</u> – a wound

<u>The 'Three Fates'</u>
    The Body-blow
    The Slow Strangler
    The Big Split

<u>The Degenerating Programme (Limping Along)</u>
    If no alternative Programme ready for power
    Usually under a Replacement Leader

<u>Dethronement</u>
    Rival Programme gets provisional hold on power

<u>Waterloo</u>
    Rival Programme gains Great Endorsement

<u>Dissolution</u>
    The Programme, now powerless, rips itself apart
    'Time of Ashes' for the host political party

In a non-democratic system, there's a similar slow access to, not a Great Endorsement but a Completed Seizure of Power. Cultural Counterblasts, of course, are soon silenced. Once things start to go wrong, there is…
    Clamping Down
    Ramping up the Rhetoric and the Violence
    Stagnation
    (Possible) Palace Revolution

The Model in Action

I'd like to show the life-cycle model I've outlined above at work. I am not claiming that the narrative below will prove that history inevitably follows my model to the letter, the way Karl Marx thought it followed his (I present my view of the scope of model-building in Appendix A). But I am confident it will be illuminating.

As I have said, there have been ten new full-on Political Programmes since the turn of the last century. These are:

- New Liberalism
- The two brief programmes of Lloyd George
- 'Tranquillity' (Inter-war Conservatism)
- 1945 Socialism
- Fifties 'One Nation' Conservatism
- 'White Heat' Modernization
- Thatcherism
- New Labour
- Populist 'Brexit' Nationalism

Here are their stories.

New Liberalism, 1906 - 1916

The end of the nineteenth century saw the rise of New Liberalism. New Liberals rejected the old, Gladstonian Liberal insistence on *laissez-faire*. At the same time, they kept their distance from Socialist thinkers, who, they considered, played down the role of the individual (politically, however, they were happy to form alliances with the rising Labour Party).

A classic Sacred Text for the Programme was Oxford philosopher TH Green's uninspiring-sounding *Lecture on Liberal Legislation and Freedom of Contract,* given in 1881. The piece went way beyond this brief, and set out a philosophy of the Liberal State. For Green, the clash between state and individual, at the heart of the Victorian Liberal idea, was often false. Rather than threatening the freedom of the individual, the state had the capacity to enable the individual by combating darker, more insidious enemies of freedom: appalling housing, overlong working hours in unsafe factories, lack of education. By fighting these constraints, it could create the circumstances in which every individual was free (in Green's words) 'to make the best of themselves': to flourish spiritually, emotionally and intellectually as well as economically. Green's model of 'making the best' was linked to an obscure concept of 'eternal consciousness', but his politics work perfectly well without this (as long as one takes a reasonably optimistic view of human nature). Green's worldview is, in fact, oddly contemporary, chiming with humanistic psychology. Substitute 'eternal consciousness' with Maslow's Hierarchy of Needs; talk about 'empowerment' – and we have a very modern philosophy.

Two more key texts were the surveys which came out around the turn of the century, and which did away with the old Liberal (and existing Conservative) view that anyone could better their lives if they worked hard and avoided obvious traps like alcohol (a view that implied that there was no point in the state creating freedom-denying and expensive institutions to give helping hands).

Charles Booth's *Life and Labour of the People of London* showed that 35% of London's population lived in extreme poverty. It did so in great detail, mapping the city and showing the levels of income on each street. In many areas, bright red shows the well-to-do living along the great arterial roads, but a few streets behind that are squares of black, the homes of the desperately poor.

Seebohm Rowntree's *Poverty, A Study of Town Life,* published in 1901, did similar work in York, where he found that about a quarter of the city's population were living in a state which he defined as not having an income 'necessary to enable families to secure the necessities of a healthy life'. Among Rowntree's poorest families, half of them had a full-time wage earner, but one who was paid so badly that the family couldn't get by. Another quarter of them suffered from the wage-earner being sick or having died. These people – together nearly 20% of the city's population – were not feckless or anti-social. They were simply trapped in poverty.

Needless to say, both these surveys were criticized by political opponents as being flawed, biased or anecdotal – *plus ça change* – but to any objective reader at the time, they were both thorough and horrifying. A rising young Conservative MP called Winston Churchill said that reading Rowntree's report "fairly made my hair stand on end". The year after he made this comment, he crossed the floor of the House of Commons to join the Liberals.

The Crucible Group for New Liberalism had formed back in the 1890s. It was called The Rainbow Circle, and took its name from the tavern on Fleet Street where it held its first meetings. Leading New Liberal thinkers such as LT Hobhouse, JA Hobson, RB Haldane, Charles Trevelyan and Herbert Samuel attended, along with figures from the emerging Labour movement, including Ramsay Macdonald. (Hobhouse would subsequently write a late-arrival Sacred Text for the movement, *Liberalism*, published in 1911.)

New Liberalism arguably acquired Significant Influence when Henry Campbell-Bannerman was elected party leader in 1899. However, 'CB', as he was known, was regarded by many as a placeholder for a younger rising star in the party, HH Asquith. It took CB time to come into his own as a Leader. A brave speech against the conduct of the Boer War in June 1901, where he condemned the 'methods of barbarism' used by the British Army (these included scorched earth policies and concentration camps), made everyone sit up and take notice of this previously quiet Scot – the moment, perhaps, of his real acquisition of influence.

The Programme had had its First Taste of Power in 1905, when the previous administration of Arthur Balfour collapsed. King Edward VII asked CB to form a minority government. The Tories thought it would be short-lived and that they would soon be back in power (a Degenerating Programme's standard reaction to an opponent's First Taste of Power).

The Liberals went to the country in 1906 with a list of Core Policies. Free Trade and Home Rule for Ireland were carried forward from Gladstonian Liberalism, but their Big New Idea was domestic. In Germany, Chancellor Bismarck had introduced a basic Welfare State in the 1880s: old-age pensions, unemployment insurance, health insurance, and free school meals. The New Liberals sought to do the same in Britain. Our 'Welfare State 1.0'.

The 1906 election resulted in a landslide win for the New Liberals: 129 seats, a Great Endorsement for the Programme. When the new parliament opened, the defeated Balfour (who had lost his seat, but had hurriedly been found another one) began an old-fashioned speech, long on cleverness and rhetorical devices but short on policy, CB interrupted. "Enough of this tomfoolery!" There was work to be done.

Acts were passed to encourage local authorities to give children free meals, to remove the rule that made trade unions liable for employers' loss of income during strikes, and to give compensation for workplace injuries. The Programme's budget introduced progressive taxation to prepare for planned bigger, more expensive reforms – the Programme, in its Pomp, could take its time.

Sadly, the health of CB and his wife both began to suffer, and the Programme's first Leader ended up having to hand over to Asquith. Asquith has gone down in history as a great PM, but he was haughty and decidedly illiberal in at least one major policy area, that of female suffrage (CB had been a supporter of that cause, but had felt he would not be able to get the measure passed in parliament). He was lucky to have a great Foil, David Lloyd George, who became Chancellor in April 1908.

The Big Wins continued to flow. 1908 saw the introduction of old-age pensions, for the over 70s. At the other end of life, a 'Children's Charter' protected the poorest children from various kinds of exploitation. In 1909, labour exchanges were set up, to simplify the process whereby the unemployed could find jobs and where expanding employers could find workers. The 1909 Housing and Town Planning Act stopped the building of any more slums. The 1911 National Insurance Act created both sick pay and unemployment benefit: to qualify, one had to pay 4d a week into a fund, which the government and employers both then topped up.

By later standards, these measures were insufficient – especially when the Great Depression of the 1930s struck. The benefits weren't universal: many people fell through the net, and the sickness and unemployment benefits only lasted 26 and 15 weeks respectively. Not many people made it to 70 then, either. But at the time these changes were regarded with horror by both Conservatives and old-fashioned Gladstonian Liberals as dangerously radical. A Political Programme has to be judged in relation to its era.

In order to pay for these things, Lloyd George introduced his 'People's Budget' of 1909. The Conservatives had sought to raise revenue through import tariffs. The free-trade Liberals sought to do so by taxing higher incomes and profits on land deals. The Conservatives, massively outvoted in the Commons, decided to fight this in the Lords, where they had a majority. This was unconstitutional – the Upper House was allowed to amend, but not reject, a financial bill. The Lords rejected it anyway. The result was a constitutional standoff, which lasted for over a year until the Lords eventually caved in. This was the Big Battle for the Programme. Asquith and Lloyd George cemented their victory with the 1911 Parliament Act, which took away the Lords' power to veto any bill. Big Battles have to be fought to the end.

The Programme arguably had its Crowning Glory with the enormous success of the 1908 London Olympics, where Britain came top of the medals table by a mile. However, the event was marred by rows between the American team and the hosts – and were the games a celebration of New Liberalism or something more atavistic and nationalist? Lord Desborough, who had been the driving force behind their organization, was a lapsed Gladstonian Liberal who had crossed the floor to the Tories some years back.

More obviously in tune with the Programme's radicalism was the rise of modernism in high culture. This was a rejection of traditions of all kinds and their replacement with emotional intensity, innovation and experiment. It was optimistic – old shackles were going to be thrown off and people would find more freedom to grow (that ultimate New Liberal value) in their creative, intellectual and personal lives. Technology would play its part: early modernists were excited by fast cars and aeroplanes, not just by ideas and art. (After World War One, Modernism became bleaker, but in the New Liberal era, modernists were bright adventurers.)

A classic mixing-ground of New Liberal ideas and modernist culture was the magazine *The English Review,* founded in 1908, the year of Asquith's accession to power, by novelist and critic Ford Madox Hueffer (who later changed his surname to Ford). A classic meeting place for the two was the residence of Lady Ottoline Morrell in Bloomsbury – her husband was Liberal MP Philip Morrell.

Looking back on the time, Virginia Woolf, a member of that set, would write, 'On or around December 1910, human character changed.' She was being deliberately provocative with that precision, but her basic point was that, just as New Liberalism had swept away the hierarchy and passivity of the previous Programme, a new sensibility of 'sunshine and fresh air' had quickly entered the nation's life.

However, there was a strong Counterblast. Many more people read the expanding, and strongly Conservative, popular press, the *Daily Mail* and the *Daily Express*, than *The English Review,* or even the Liberal *Manchester Guardian*. Rudyard Kipling, who had won the Nobel Prize for Literature in 1907, was a vociferous opponent of Home Rule for Ireland, as epitomized in his 1912 rant, *Ulster*.

The New Liberal Programme had a long Pomp. (Its huge electoral majority vanished in 1910, but thanks to the loyal support of Southern Irish MPs it retained its parliamentary power.)

In 1912, it managed a Great Escape when almost all its key players were caught up in a scandal involving insider trading in the Marconi Company. Shares had been bought just before the announcement of a government contract. Asquith was not involved, and backed his team members who had been implicated. The furore died down.

Slow Stranglers were beginning to emerge, however. Suffragism grew ever more militant, and the official reaction to it ever more oppressive. Asquith refused to countenance electoral reform – a classic example of a Programme being threatened by a blind spot in its Worldview (or, in this case, the Worldview of its Leader).

Ireland became ever more polarized, with Gladstonian moves towards Home Rule being matched by rising militancy in Ulster. In 1914, British forces even threatened to mutiny if told to fire on Ulster militia.

However, neither of these ended up destroying the Programme. Historian Lord Morgan writes that the Liberal government 'was still powerful in 1914'. It was working on reforms, and still had what Morgan calls 'the zest to govern'.

What destroyed it was war, and the change of national mood that went with it. On the 28th June of that year, the Archduke Franz Ferdinand made an official visit to Sarajevo...

Neither Asquith nor Lloyd George wanted war. After the Archduke's assassination, the former had written that there was 'no reason why we should be anything more than spectators' in any resulting European conflict. The latter had added that 'there are always clouds in the international sky'. But once Asquith had rejected the idea of officially promising not to take part in such a conflict, events spiralled out of control, and war duly broke out, 37 days after the killing.

Arguably that was the Programme's last Great Escape. War was not greeted with dismay or resignation but by a rush of patriotic fervour – and the popular belief that, given Britain's military and naval might, it would 'all be over by Christmas'.

It wasn't, of course. The first Big Failure (hardly the fault of the Programme, but the first major divergence between its plan and reality) came when the numerically superior Russians, who had been expected to sweep into Germany from the East, were trounced at the Battle of Tannenberg, an event graphically described in Alexander Solzhenitsyn's *August 1914*.

In September, the armies on the Western front began building trenches. By Christmas, these extended from the Channel to the Swiss Alps. This was the Body-blow to the Programme, born in a time of peace but now an irrelevance in a brand new world of mass slaughter by machine-gun and war by attrition.

By the start of 1915, the Programme was already Degenerating fast.

Things came to a head in May 1915 after the Battle of Aubers Ridge, near Béthune, where a British offensive achieved nothing and over 11,000 men were killed or wounded (the Germans lost less than 1,000). A shortage of shells was blamed for the disaster. Asquith concluded that the Liberals could not govern alone and asked the Conservatives to form a Coalition. The Conservatives agreed – ironically, one of their conditions for this was that the then still Liberal Winston Churchill should be removed from the Cabinet. The new government took over on 25th May. This marked the Dethronement of the New Liberal Programme. It no longer controlled events or chimed with the national mood, though, as it was nominally still in power, could still be blamed if things went wrong.

In 1916, the progress of the war went from bad to worse, with the collapse of the Gallipoli campaign in January, the disaster of Kut-al-Amara on the Mesopotamian front, in April, and the carnage at the Somme on July 1st.

Asquith's personal star faded, too. In September 1916 his eldest son, Raymond, was killed at the Battle of Flers–Courcelette. His difficulties with alcohol escalated (our word 'squiffy' comes from him). On the political front, he faced more and more dilemmas, as the war required ever more illiberal moves such as the introduction of conscription. The popular press had it in for him. In December of that dreadful year, the once-mighty all-reforming New Liberal Programme met its Waterloo, being put out of its misery by the man who had once been one of its driving forces, Lloyd George.

The Dissolution of the Programme followed. In the 1918 election, Asquith's section of a by then long-split party won a measly 36 seats. This number didn't include Asquith, who lost his.

New Liberalism

Original Leader: Henry Campbell-Bannerman (CB)

Leader: Herbert Asquith

Foil: David Lloyd George (Chancellor)

The Villain: Poverty

The New Future: Freedom for everyone to fulfil themselves

Core Policies: 'Welfare State 1.0', Free Trade, Home Rule for Ireland

Crucible Group: Rainbow Circle

Sacred Texts: *Lecture on Liberal Legislation and Freedom of Contract* (TH Green), Booth and Rowntree reports, *Liberalism* (Hobhouse)

Gaining Significant Influence: CB becomes party leader 1899 / his 'methods of barbarism' speech, 1901

First Taste of Power: Minority government of 1905

Great Endorsement: 129 seat victory in 1906

Crowning Glory: (?) 1908 Olympics

Cultural Endorsement: Modernism, *The English Review*

Cultural Counterblasts: The popular press, *Ulster* (Kipling)

Big Wins: Introduction of welfare measures, 'People's budget'

Big Battle: With House of Lords

Great Escapes: Marconi Scandal, outbreak of war

Slow Stranglers (in peacetime): Ireland, suffragette movement

First Big Failure: German victory on Eastern front, August 1914

Body-blows: Trenches on the Western front, the emerging nature of the War, Battle of Aubers Ridge

Dethronement: Entering Coalition, May 1915

Waterloo: Lloyd George becomes PM, December 1916

Lloyd George 1
The Knock-out Blow: 1916 to 1918

It took nearly 2½ years, from the assassination of the unfortunate Archduke to the Waterloo of the old peacetime New Liberal Programme, for a true war-winning alternative to take power.

'Take power' is what it did. The electorate could not speak in the middle of the conflict, so the change came via a Palace Revolution – or (as this model predicts) by two such revolutions. The first dethroned the struggling old Programme, but still in a way that the new Programme's grasp on power was provisional. The second fully and irrevocably installed the new one.

The first Palace Revolution, detailed in the last section, took place in May 1915. After it, Asquith was still PM, but now as leader of a Coalition. Never a war leader – he was assiduous but lacked the bravado necessary at such a time – he was no longer the centre of energy, which is what a Programme Leader must be. That was now his former Foil, David Lloyd George. In the new administration, the Welshman was made Minister of Munitions. Munitions had previously been the responsibility of the military: Lloyd George seized control and piled in with his usual vigour, getting industrialists involved and encouraging the employment of women in the munitions factories (he promised them the vote in return, a Core pledge that he duly honoured). There were no more shell shortages.

Elsewhere, however, endless mishaps, mentioned in the previous section, befell the old Degenerating Programme.

December 1916 saw various political manoeuvrings, led by Lloyd George (who had been made Secretary of State for War in June), Tory leader Andrew Bonar Law and newspaper proprietor Max Aitken. The Conservatives refused to serve under Asquith any longer. He resigned, and a new Coalition was formed, with some Liberals, the Conservatives and Labour (who were persuaded to join by a speech from Lloyd George). On the 7th of that month, the 'cottage-born' Welshman became PM.

This second Palace Revolution was the equivalent of an electoral Great Endorsement. From then on, Lloyd George had all the power he needed, to do whatever he (and his new Programme) wanted – within the UK, of course. On the fields of Flanders or the high seas, he had less control, though he battled with the top brass over strategy (Asquith's approach had been to let the military men run things as they thought fit).

The new Programme was utterly different from its predecessor. Its Big New Idea was brutally simple: to fight the war to the end and win it with 'a knock-out blow', whatever the cost. If Lloyd George, the former great New Liberal Chancellor, was its Leader, its tone and its parliamentary muscle came from the Conservatives. The War Cabinet that he formed featured three Conservatives, a Socialist and himself: not an Asquithian Liberal in sight. That didn't mean that Lloyd George instantly lost his spiky radicalism, but it did mean that it was focused in a new direction. The war became a moral crusade, a fight against the absolute evil instantiated by the Kaiser's Germany. Only total defeat could expunge such evil – and result in the end of war forever, as the forces of virtue would have won.

The Programme had had no time for a Crucible Group. Lloyd George did the next best thing, and formed a virtual one on acceding to power, a group of close advisors that became known as his 'Garden Suburb'. This was a small collection of diverse talents (which is what Crucible Groups should be): a diplomat, an academic, two Welsh MPs, a plutocrat and the Welsh wizard himself.

A few days after this martial, determined new Programme seized power, the Germans made a peace offer to the allies via US President Woodrow Wilson. It was couched in haughty terms and was probably unacceptable – but it is an interesting debate as to what might have happened if it had been made, not to the Leader of a Programme right at the start of its Pomp, but instead to an older, Degenerating administration not wedded to total war. Such an administration could have used the offer as a starting-point for negotiations. Had these been successful and a peace been achieved, there would have been no Passchendaele. There might have been no Russian Revolution. There would probably have been no Spanish flu, which was spread by troop movements and preyed on a people weakened by war. There would certainly have been no Treaty of Versailles. Adolf Hitler would have most likely been an irate nobody, ranting at anybody who would listen – till they got bored – in downmarket Munich beer cellars. But that is speculation. The offer was refused, and the war ground on – and on and on.

There was no massive Cultural Endorsement of the new Programme (the patriotic 'In Flanders Fields' was written in 1915). The administration and its supporters spewed out propaganda: Germany represented absolute evil and we were fighting for absolute good. (A fiction, of course, but one that would ring true in the conflict that followed a generation later: one wonders how much this stuff was a self-fulfilling prophecy.)

Much more lasting was the Counterblast produced by the great anti-war poets of the era, civilized, sensitive young men horrified by the mechanized brutality of the Western Front.

The Programme can claim a number of Big Wins. At home, the economy was put on a war footing, ending the delusion, of the old Programme, that this was an old-fashioned war that could be fought with little domestic disruption (there had been some piecemeal intervention in the economy by the previous Programme, but the new one took this to a new level. For example, by the end of the war the government bought and distributed 80% of the nation's food.) In 1918, the Programme finally laid the ghost of Asquith and introduced female suffrage.

Also unlike Asquith, Lloyd George intervened in military strategy. Most historians say these interventions were successful (some say he should have intervened more, for example sacking Haig in early 1917, before the Passchendaele campaign, which Lloyd George later described as 'senseless'). His insistence on the convoy system for Atlantic merchant shipping, against the desires of the Admiralty, neutered the U-boats that, in early 1917, had threatened to starve the country. When the German Army threatened to break through the Western front in early 1918, he forced the military to accept a unified overall command.

But, of course, the real Big Win, and the only one that truly mattered, came at 11.00 on 11th November, 1918. The knock-out blow had been delivered.

Lloyd George 1
The Knock-out Blow

Leader: David Lloyd George

Villain: Germany

The New Future: Winning 'the war to end all wars'

Core Policies: No negotiation with Germany. Centralized state power, including of LG over military

First Taste of Power: Coalition, May 1915

Great Endorsement: Palace Revolution of December 1916

Crucible Group (post-victory): the 'Garden Suburb'

Cultural Endorsement: Not much. Propaganda

Cultural Counterblasts: The great War Poets

Big Battle: With Germany

Big Wins: Creating a genuine war economy, Atlantic convoy system, unified command, votes for women – and, finally, Victory

Crowning Glory: Victory celebrations, 1918

Lloyd George 2
'A Fit Country for Heroes to Live in', 1918 - 22

Normally a Political Programme never quits in the middle of its Pomp. Why would it? But with the war won, this one had achieved its aim. Just as there had been in August 1914, there was a whole new world to deal with.

The Leader of the old Programme used the huge national support he had to create a second one. This had its own Big New Idea, 'to make Britain a fit country for heroes to live in'.

An election was held as soon as possible after the armistice. The tone changed during the campaign, with initial, optimistic Liberalism giving way to an angrier determination to 'squeeze the German lemon until the pips squeak' (a stump quote from a Conservative, Eric Geddes, which Lloyd George took on). This reversion to Triumphalism was a bad omen for the Programme. Who was really going to call the shots? Political Programmes may tweak their messages during election campaigns, but they don't introduce, then prioritize, radically new themes.

The change worked in the short term, however. Lloyd George's Coalition received a massive Endorsement – one that made the 1906 landslide look like a gentle nod of approval. However, the majority was a 'Coalition Conservative' one. Led by Bonar Law but accepting 'the man who won the war' as PM, the Conservatives had 332 seats. Those Liberals who supported Lloyd George (the 'Coalition Liberals') had only 127. Labour was the next biggest party with 57. The old

Asquithian Liberals won just 36. Almost all of Southern Ireland voted for the new, more radically separatist party of Sinn Fein, who refused to sit in the Commons. The Coalition had huge power – but to do what, exactly?

It set out, as planned, with a Liberal agenda. The school leaving age was raised to 14. An act subsidised local authorities to build houses – a leap forward, as housebuilding had not been seen as a government responsibility before. National Insurance was extended to more workers. Former New Liberal Christopher Addison was made Minister of Health, a new position charged with improving public wellbeing. Old-age pensions were increased, and offered to blind people over 50. Working hours were reduced.

The issue of Ireland, an old Liberal cause, was finally settled. The road to that settlement was bloody in the extreme, with what was effectively a war between the IRA and British forces breaking out in 1919. But Lloyd George managed to negotiate an agreement between the furious antagonists – something that none of his predecessors had been able to do. Despite the bloodshed before the agreement and the fact that it still had to be finalized (bitter disputes remained about the precise boundaries of the two Irelands), some historians regard this as his finest achievement.

The PM's negotiating skills were less in evidence in the lead-up to the Treaty of Versailles. Despite his Triumphalism at the election, he had a nuanced understanding of the situation, writing in private: 'If she [Germany] feels she has been unjustly treated… she will find means of exacting retribution from her conquerors'. However he encountered a French delegation as greedy for vengeance as his own public self and an American one with unrealistically high ideals (which was soon ignored), and ended up signing a treaty that he must have known in his heart would be disastrous. Despite this, he was welcomed as a hero returning from the negotiations. This, surely, qualifies as a Great Escape, a grievous policy mistake not picked up on at the time.

On the home front, there was a brief boom in 1919, but this was accompanied by soaring inflation. This then turned to a bust, with the number of unemployed rocketing. Time for the Programme to fully show its Liberal colours and support these people…

The popular press and the Conservatives began insisting the expensive reforms be turned back and the nation's books balanced. Given the parliamentary arithmetic, Lloyd George had no option but to agree. Addison was sacked. Eric Geddes, of 'squeeze the pips' fame, was brought in to make cuts. These were swingeing, and became known as the 'Geddes Axe'. The Axe cut the Liberal heart out of the Programme. It was the Programme's Body-blow, its fatal U-turn.

The Programme was now Degenerating. Accusations of corruption surfaced: honours had been sold to fund a future new party (a peerage would set you back over £50,000). Lloyd George was offered a massive advance for his memoirs, which people considered an insult to war victims. The final straw was a crisis in Turkey. Turkish troops were advancing on Chanak, a British outpost in the north-west of the country. Lloyd George wanted to go to war to defend it (as did Churchill). Some Liberals and most Conservatives did not, and in the end, a peaceful settlement was negotiated. Lloyd George had lost the last of his authority over the administration. The Coalition fell apart.

An election was called, which the Conservatives won by a healthy-looking majority. That majority was not to last, but the Liberal Party would not be the winner next time round – or ever again (at time of writing, anyway). Ironically, the Liberals had the two most influential political thinkers of the era that followed, John Maynard Keynes and William Beveridge, in its ranks – which shows, sadly, that having great individual thinkers is not a sufficient condition of political success.

The relatively short life of this Programme also shows that it takes more than a Leader, however charismatic, to create a lasting Political Programme. There is talk of modern British politics becoming more 'presidential'. This chapter is a reminder that this is not new – and that our previous experiment with such politics did not last long.

After losing the 1922 election, Lloyd George tried to reunite the Liberals, but Asquith and his supporters had had enough of him. As a back-bencher, he returned to his more radical self. The Liberal Party continued its Dissolution.

Lloyd George 2
'A Fit Country for Heroes to Live in'

Leader: David Lloyd George
Core Policy: Continuing expansion of Welfare State
The Great Endorsement: Massive Coalition victory in 1918 election
Big Wins: Early 'New Liberal' measures, initial post-war boom,
  a settlement in Ireland
Great Escape: Conceding too much to the French at Versailles
Slow Strangler: Lack of parliamentary majority for LG's ideas
Body-blow: 'Geddes Axe'
Dethronement: Conservatives quit the Coalition, October 1922
Waterloo: Conservative landslide, 1924

Tranquillity, 1922 - 1940

The Conservative Party has long been the master of self-reinvention. It had been out for blood between 1914 and 1918. In 1922, reacting to the general feeling of war exhaustion and, in particular, Lloyd George's militaristic response to Chanak, it recreated itself as the bringer of peace. 'We should have tranquillity and stability both at home and abroad,' said Andrew Bonar Law in his election address. In the model proposed in this book, such reinvention is a good thing. A Political Programme has to be responsive to current needs and consistent with itself, not consistent with old, used-up Programmes from the past.

Reinvention is never, and should never be, total. Some traditional Tory themes were retained. Taxes, which Bonar Law described as 'the greatest clog on industry', would be kept low. He concluded: 'The nation's first need… is, in every walk of life, to get on with its work with the minimum of interference at home and of disturbance abroad.'

There does not seem to have been a Crucible Group for this Programme. The nearest approach, perhaps, is a meeting at the Carlton Club held in October 1922, when the party's MPs met to decide whether to ditch the Coalition with the Lloyd George Liberals after the Chanak Crisis. After a particularly impressive speech by Stanley Baldwin, they voted to do so. The policy manifesto was written in some haste after that – but proved very durable.

Similarly, there is no powerful Canon for the Programme – though when I think of it, I am reminded of Conservative philosopher Edmund Burke's lines, written back in 1790: "Because half a dozen grasshoppers under a fern make the field ring with their importunate chink, whilst thousands of great cattle, reposed beneath the shadow of the British oak, chew the cud and are silent, pray do not imagine that those who make the noise are the only inhabitants of the field.".

Baldwin, the man who would end up as the Programme Leader, was a not a theorist but a practical businessman with a streak of rural romanticism and a strong Christian faith. Of all the Leaders in this story, he is the least personally ambitious. He went into politics out of a sense of duty. When politicians start talking about their eagerness to serve the public, everyone else usually groans, but in Baldwin's case this really was the motivation. He was lucky, too, of course. He didn't have to scramble up the first part of the greasy pole. His father, Alfred, had been an MP and had died young; Stanley was expected to step into his shoes and duly did so. He then found he was rather good at politics, like a child gifted an old guitar who turns out to have a real talent for songwriting.

The Carlton Club meeting can be seen as the moment of the Programme's gaining Significant Influence. The election win, the First Taste of Power for the new Programme, followed almost immediately afterwards, in November.

The majority of the win – 74 seats – might look like an instant Great Endorsement. But it wasn't. Things don't usually work that fast. The party was still recovering from its relationship with the tempestuous Lloyd George. The man who had led the party to its new victory, Bonar Law, was in poor health, and Baldwin, who soon replaced him, had to learn the game quickly. He did, but not quickly enough. Rather than tough out a potentially party-splitting plan to ditch Free Trade and return to the old policy of tariffs and 'imperial preference', he decided to go to the polls – and lost his majority. David Cameron's attempt to mend his party's split over Europe by holding a referendum leaps to mind as a modern parallel.

A new Aspirant Programme then got its First Taste of Power, but failed to translate that into a Great Endorsement. This wasn't just the First Taste of Power for a new Programme but for a new party: Labour. However, it was not a success. Given the parliamentary arithmetic – it did not win a majority – it had very little chance of so being. All the Programme's leader, Ramsay Macdonald, could do was show that his new party could govern responsibly and aim for a proper Endorsement at a future election. It made some progress, domestically via the Wheatley Act that mandated the building of more social housing, and abroad via attempts to calm the continuing French determination to crucify Germany. But it was always going to need a proper mandate, and after ten months, it asked the electorate for one. Its request was not granted. Baldwin returned, now with his own Great Endorsement, a massive 210 seat majority.

It was as if he had never left. The 'Tranquillity' Programme was calmly reinstated and government went on as in 1922/3, though now in its Pomp.

The Programme enjoyed its Crowning Glory at the British Empire Exhibition of 1924/5 (part of the Expo ran during the Macdonald administration, but it had been a child of the Tranquillity Programme and was a perfect expression of it). Visitors – adults paid 1/6, children 9d – could stroll round the huge site in Wembley and visit opulent 'Palaces' of Industry, Engineering and Arts and Pavilions from 56 territories in the Empire (the one from Canada featured a statue of the Prince of Wales carved from butter). They could enjoy the boating lake, funfair and numerous restaurants. The tone of the exhibition was imperialist, but, in tune with 'Tranquillity', it celebrated an Empire that worked amicably together. There were no Maxim guns on display.

The Programme had a strong Cultural Endorsement. The model figure of the era was the gentleman, a role epitomized by Baldwin himself. The idea was never quite thought through, however. In theory, a true gentleman – like a Baldwin voter – could come from any class. He was polite, listened to others' views, didn't score cheap points off anyone and took others' interests into consideration when acting. If he had an advantage, social or physical, he never used it unfairly or maliciously. The lady by his side was similar.

However, in practice the notion was tied up with upper middle-class snobbery. The gents in the popular literature of the time all came from this stratum. In Warwick Deeping's 1925 bestseller *Sorrell and Son,* an impoverished army officer, returned from the trenches, makes huge sacrifices to ensure his son has the education that will make him a gentleman. Gents in popular thrillers, from the rather decent Richard Hannay to the racist thug Bulldog Drummond, were all quite posh (full-on aristos were a bit suspect), though often, like Captain Stephen Sorrell MC, short of cash.

Ladies do not come well out of *Sorrell and Son* or the adventures of Bulldog Drummond, but find a more sympathetic niche in the era's 'Golden Age' detective stories, where their superior understanding of human nature enables them to solve crimes that baffle blundering, fact-bound male police officers.

At a more highbrow level, Baldwin's own sensibilities were mirrored by Georgian poets such as John Drinkwater and John Masefield. The

Georgian movement had begun before the Great War, but reached the apex of its popularity during the Baldwin years. The poems are formally correct: they rhyme and scan. They are romantic, outdoors-y, slightly wistful and very English. The work of Ralph Vaughan Williams has a similar sense. *The Lark Ascending* has to be Baldwinism set to music.

Counterblasts came mainly from writers on the left like WH Auden and Stephen Spender, especially as the 1920s turned into the 1930s: novelist/critic DJ Taylor refers to the 1930s as 'the Pink Decade'. George Orwell's *The Road to Wigan Pier*, published in 1937, showed that despite Baldwin's genuine intentions to heal the class divide, his Programme hadn't done nearly enough. The PM's vision, formed in his family's paternalistic (and extremely successful) medium-size provincial ironworks, didn't map onto the nation as a whole, where entire sectors were in decline and old class antagonisms ran deep.

A few other writers, like poet Ezra Pound, had equal contempt for Baldwinian gentlemanliness but veered off to the far right.

In 1925, the Programme scored its first Big Win by sorting out the borders of the new Northern Ireland. This was a fraught issue, with a very real threat of a return to violence if negotiations failed. Baldwin, like Lloyd George, was a skilled negotiator, and masterminded a settlement acceptable to both sides. He wrote 'pax pacem' in the Chequers visitors' book (where the negotiations had been held) after the participants had left.

On the international front, the same year saw Britain sign the Treaty of Locarno, establishing Germany's Western borders and effectively readmitting Germany, now under the liberal Weimar republic, to the family of nations. Tranquillity could now reign in Europe, too.

An early Great Escape was the return to the gold standard, a measure that kept the pound at a fixed rate that was far too high, which made British goods hard to sell abroad. However, the electorate did not punish this, and the move would be reversed in 1931.

The Programme's Big Battle? This was the General Strike of 1926, fought against left-wing, unionized labour.

Baldwin did the fighting in his own way. In his 1924 election victory speech, he spoke of his ambition 'to make one nation of our own people which, if secured, nothing else matters in the world'. (The slogan 'one nation' is often attributed to Victorian Conservative PM Benjamin Disraeli, but 'Dizzy' never used it: it was Baldwin who first did so.) Baldwin divided his opponents, making a distinction between the dispute with the miners which had started it off, which he settled with negotiations, and the wider strike, which he saw as an expression of unacceptable extremism, 'an attempt to take over the function of the Government by a body that has not been elected'.

On the day the strike collapsed, Baldwin broadcast to the nation: "Our business is not to triumph over those who have failed in a mistaken attempt." Baldwin didn't do Triumphalism. Instead, he chatted calmly and reasonably to listeners to the ever more popular radio, as if he were sitting in an armchair next to them, puffing away at his pipe.

In 1929, it was time for another election. Baldwin campaigned with a suitably tranquil slogan, 'Safety First'. Essentially, what happened was a re-run of 1922/4. The electorate decided Baldwin was a bit dull, voted for someone else, but soon changed its mind.

The result of the 1929 election was a First Taste of Power for a second

Aspirant Labour Programme. It had no outright majority, but (unlike in 1922) was the biggest party in the House. A minority government was duly sworn in, and set about a programme of public works.

They were appallingly unlucky. The election was held in May. On October 24th, the previously booming US stock market suffered a major sell-off. The Wall Street Crash had begun. The global Depression would follow. The economy went into a slump. Unemployment began to soar. A Committee set up under Sir George May, former Secretary of Prudential Insurance, recommended massive cuts to government expenditure. (Keynes said it was 'the most foolish document I ever had the misfortune to read' – but people weren't listening to him.) Just as Lloyd George had done in 1922, the new Aspirant Labour Programme did a violent U-turn and followed May's advice – a self-inflicted Body-blow. The party split, something that no minority administration can afford to do.

Macdonald, still Labour leader, tried to form a National Government with the Conservatives. He was pressurized into testing this new administration at the polls, now standing against his old party (something that has never been forgiven by the left). In the 1931 election, the National Government won a massive majority of 497. A victory for Macdonald? Almost all the 'National' candidates were Conservatives, and they called the tune. They did so in a suitably tranquil way, of course. Baldwin liked Macdonald and was happy to work with him. But when illness forced Macdonald to retire in 1935, who else was there to step into his shoes, but the man who had effectively been in charge all along? Back to business as usual.

That business seemed largely successful. There was growing prosperity in south and central England. Light engineering flourished and more people moved into higher-paid, salaried work. The Programme's real Big Win was the suburbia that sprawled out from Britain's major cities, where millions of a newly well-off middle-class folk genuinely found leafy-laned tranquillity.

However, Slow Stranglers were also at work.

If parts of Britain were flourishing, others weren't. The era of Baldwin's Programme has become associated with poverty, exemplified by the Jarrow march of 1936, which was the culmination of years of underemployment in a declining industry, shipbuilding. The Programme seemed to have no remedy for this.

An even more vicious Strangler was the Programme's inability to deal with the rising threat of fascism. It is a core theme of this book that, as events never stand still, Political Programmes, which can't change their core beliefs and policies without becoming meaningless, are doomed to become outdated. This happened to Tranquillity with particular viciousness.

In the mid-1930s, the two European fascist states both started pushing at the established international order.

During 1935, Mussolini steadily increased military pressure on Ethiopia (then called Abyssinia). The League of Nations did nothing of substance to stop him. In October of that year, he invaded. Britain and France undermined what efforts the League had been making to punish Italy by trying to do a deal with the invaders. After a lull over the Christmas period, hostilities were stepped up. A key battle was the capture of the strategically important mountain of Ambra Aradam on 19th February 1936. Mustard gas was sprayed on the fleeing Ethiopians.

Hitler, who had been quietly observing the proceedings, noted the world's response (or lack of it) to this, and marched into the Rhineland on March 5th. This was in direct contravention of the Treaty of Versailles. Again, nothing was done.

In retrospect, letting the dictators do this was disastrous. But there was little popular or elite support for military action at that time, in the UK or in the country with whom this standing up would have jointly to be done, France. These have to qualify as 'Great Escapes': policy mistakes that went unpunished at the time.

It wasn't till mid-1937 that Labour's National Executive finally agreed to stop voting against defence expenditure. The claim, later made, that the bulldog British people were eager for war in the late 1930s but doddering old Baldwin refused to listen, is grossly unfair. The vast majority desperately wanted peace and Baldwin simply stuck to the values of his Programme (created, remember, as a response to the excessive militarism of an earlier era) – which is what all Political Programme Leaders do.

Fascism, Naziism and Soviet Communism represented totally new Worldviews and Action Plans that decent democrats like Baldwin (and most of his contemporaries) were completely unable to comprehend. Arguably, they could have done: the Nazi Sacred Text, *Mein Kampf*, had been available in an abridged translation since 1933. But such is the tunnel vision of Political Programmes: a blessing at their start, a curse at their end. And before we judge too harshly – even post-COP26, are we being just as complacent about the Climate Emergency right now?

Baldwin retired due to ill health in May 1937, leaving in what diarist Harold Nicholson called a 'blaze of affection'. A Replacement Leader,

Neville Chamberlain, took over. Chamberlain was a lesser man than Baldwin: spiky and distant, an effective minister but a poor PM.

Mussolini completed his occupation of Ethiopia: now it was Hitler's turn to keep upping the ante. March 1938 saw the annexation of Austria and his preparations to invade Czechoslovakia. The latter were briefly held up by the Munich agreement of September 1938, signed by Germany, Britain, France and Italy, which ceded the German-speaking parts of that country to Hitler. The agreement was generally praised in Britain. A by-election in Oxford that October was won by a pro-Munich candidate.

The nature of Hitler's domestic policies could no longer be hidden after *Kristallnacht* in November of that year, when SA and Hitler Youth members went on a national rampage, vandalizing Jewish properties and killing Jewish citizens, while the SS rounded up tens of thousands more Jews and put them in camps. In March 1939, the nature of the Führer's military plans became equally obvious as he ripped up Chamberlain's piece of paper and invaded the rest of Czechoslovakia. All his previous military aggression had been aimed at drawing ethnically German areas into the national fold. This took his aggressiveness to a new level.

The viciousness of *Kristallnacht* and the invasion of non-German-speaking Czechoslovakia were joint Body-blows to the Programme. The world was no longer tranquil, and now everyone could see this.

The now-Degenerating Programme limped along for a year after this. Chamberlain was forced to declare war in September 1939 after Germany's next act of international aggression, against Poland. He was ousted in a Palace Revolution in May 1940: the Programme's

Dethronement (more about this in the next chapter).

The Tranquillity Programme met its Waterloo almost at once, as it became the butt of vicious and sustained criticism. The book *Guilty Men* appeared in July 1940, which shredded the reputations of 24 'appeasers'. Baldwin was one of them. The Programme's Dissolution began. Its reputation has yet to recover.

Tranquillity

Leader: Stanley Baldwin

Villain: Class politics, especially Bolshevism

The New Future: Quiet economic growth

Core Policies: Tariffs, peace treaties in Europe, moderate the class struggle

Gaining Significant Influence: Exiting Coalition, October 1922

The First Taste of Power: Election victory, November 1922

The Great Endorsement: 1924 election, 210 majority

Crowning Glory: British Empire Exhibition 1924/5

Great Escapes: Going onto gold standard, 1925; insufficient reply to aggression by Mussolini and Hitler, 1935/6

Cultural Endorsement: *Sorrell and Son*, Warwick Deeping, 1925

Counterblast: *The Road to Wigan Pier,* George Orwell, 1937

Big Wins: Irish border settled, Locarno Treaty, suburbia

Big Battle: General strike, 1926

Body-blows: *Kristallnacht*, 1938; Hitler invades Czechoslovakia, 1939

Slow Stranglers: Failure to address poverty, failure to understand Fascism/Naziism

Dethronement: Churchill/Attlee Coalition, May 1940

Waterloo: Publication of *Guilty Men*, July 1940

1945 Socialism, 1940 - 1951

I've called this Programme 1945 Socialism, because 1945 was its *annus mirabilis*, the year of its Great Endorsement. But it was the major force in the land from May 1940 onwards. The idea that the 1945 election landslide emerged out of nowhere is a myth. Britain was in many ways already a socialist state by then, and had been for five years.

I nearly called this Programme 'Patriotic Communalism', a term used by historian Lord Peter Hennessy. It was certainly both these things. The first is often forgotten. Clement Attlee and his government were fiercely patriotic, in a way that would make the modern 'woke' left, or even woke's 'right-on' 1980s precursors, squirm. When Ernest Bevin said of the atom bomb "We've got to have a bloody Union Jack on top of it", he wasn't being ironic or postmodern. He meant it. Attlee valued many traditional British institutions. A firm monarchist, he got on well with King George VI. He never disowned his public-school background, retaining a soft spot for his *alma mater*, Haileybury College.

If there was a Crucible Group for the Programme, it met a long time before the Programme took office. After the electoral disaster of 1931 nearly wiped out the Labour Party, Attlee worked with George Lansbury, Stafford Cripps and a group of academics at the LSE led by Harold Laski to formulate the Action Plan. However, time – and practicality – watered down its realization; it was much more radical than the policies that were actually put into practice in 1940 or 1945.

There was no real Action Group. Attlee got involved in the Labour

Party from his youth and rose though its ranks by hard work and because people liked and trusted him. He acquired Significant Influence when he became its leader in 1935, largely because his rivals for the post had all made enemies in various parts of the party.

He then led the party for two decades. Contrary to the slurs of his detractors, Attlee was a true Leader, not just a placeholder who somehow got stuck in place. His leadership style was different to the modern one, which is why he is often underrated. He stuck quietly, but firmly and consistently, to his views, but he allowed himself to be outvoted in cabinet, not because he was weak but because he believed that was the right way to do things. His combination of solidity, utter integrity and personal modesty turned out to be a huge asset. People liked him. Unlike most successful politicians, he had very little vanity or ego.

Arguably there was a huge Canon for this Programme. Victor Gollancz' Left Book Club offered readers one title a month from 1936. But a Canon should be narrowed down to a few specific Sacred Texts.

Attlee's greatest influence was *Looking Backward* by the American writer Edward Bellamy, a story about a Rip van Winkle character who goes to sleep in the year of the book's publication, 1887, and wakes up in the year 2000, to find how much the world has changed.

Attlee's own *The Social Worker*, published in 1920, has been described by his biographer John Bew as 'the forgotten script of the twentieth-century Labour Party'. In it, he argues that the Great War had shown that everyone was involved in the life of the nation. Attlee blamed the Victorians for destroying notions of citizenship (a key concept in the 1945 Socialist Programme) and replacing it with class- or individual interest. Citizenship gave us rights but also entailed responsibilities, to rein in self-interest at certain times and work for the general good. This mindset came naturally during a war – but was also the correct one for peace. In another book, *The Labour Party in Perspective* (1937), he laid out much of the agenda that would be followed post 1945.

However, probably the most powerful Sacred Text for 1945 Socialism would be created after the Programme had achieved its First Taste of Power – and then not even by a socialist. The Beveridge Report, which came out in 1942, was written by Liberal economist William Beveridge. The report, officially titled *Social Insurance and Allied Services*, talked of 'Five Giants on the road to reconstruction': Want, Disease, Ignorance, Squalour and Idleness. It argued that these should be fought with state-driven programmes: benefits for those unable to work (including a larger old-age pension), free healthcare and education for all, a massive house-building programme and a commitment to full employment. Much more than Attlee's books, the report fired the public imagination and swung opinion behind the party determined to put its recommendations into practice, Labour.

Unlike modern manifestoes, which are treated with a certain amount of cynicism, Labour's 1945 one, *Let us Face the Future*, was also a key text. In those days, you had to buy a party manifesto if you wanted to read it – and over a million copies were sold.

But back to the 1930s… At that decade advanced, Hitler and Mussolini became more and more aggressive. Attlee found his feet as a Leader in response to this. Labour, and Attlee himself, had wavered on the subject of rearmament, but after a visit to Spain in December 1937, where he met, amongst others, the members of the Major Attlee Brigade, the Leader set a clear anti-appeasement tone. At times, he spoke louder and clearer than even Churchill.

Britain went to war in September 1939. A 'phoney war' followed, but in April 1940, Hitler invaded Denmark and Norway. The resulting crisis created the First Taste of Power for the new Programme, as a Coalition replaced the old administration. As often with First Tastes, this only came about by a close margin. Right up to, and arguably even after, the crucial 'Norway' parliamentary debate from May 7th to the 9th (best remembered for Leo Amery's telling Chamberlain "in the name of God, go" but where the major critical speech was made by Attlee), commentators expected the Chamberlain government to survive, despite the fact it was clearly limping along.

It didn't survive, of course. On the morning of May 10th, German troops flooded into the Netherlands and Belgium. Chamberlain resigned that evening. The new Coalition was not led by Attlee but by Churchill. Churchill, with his pugnacity and superb oratory, was the man to lead the country. But he led it along a route that Attlee and his supporters had designed.

Most modern Churchillians will be horrified by the thought that their hero has anything to do with the most left-wing Political Programme the UK has ever seen. But he had everything to do with it. The government that he led ran wartime Britain as a highly centralized command economy. Arguably it had no option to do otherwise, but that is what it did. Attlee was Churchill's second-in-command (he moved into 11 Downing Street). The administration had men of the left (plus the occasional woman) at the highest levels. A David Low cartoon of the time – *All behind you, Winston* – shows Churchill rolling up his sleeves and marching to war. Directly behind him are senior members of the Labour Party: Attlee, Ernest Bevin and Herbert

Morrison. Attlee often deputized for Churchill in parliament, including to announce the Emergency Powers Defence Bill, which gave sweeping powers to government of a kind more like Soviet Russia than the lost, tranquil Britain of Stanley Baldwin.

Many Conservatives thought that the Coalition was simply a temporary matter, driven by necessity. After the War, things would get back to 'normal', with a grateful nation voting for its warrior leader, the way it had done for Lloyd George in 1918. This is typical 'This won't last' thinking by an old guard during a new Programme's First Taste. Instead, the nation voted for the Political Programme that had won the War, not the individual. It did so decisively: Labour scored a landslide victory in the election of July 1945, a majority of 145. This was the Great Endorsement of Attlee's Programme.

In the same month, JB Priestley's *An Inspector Calls* was premiered, a classic Cultural Endorsement of the Programme's values. In it, a mysterious Inspector Goole quizzes a successful industrialist and his family about the suicide of a young working-class woman. They all turn out, in different ways, to have been responsible for her downfall. (The play is set in 1912, but the audience would have had the 1930s clearly in their minds.)

More generally, the new Programme's cultural Heroes and Heroines were not Tranquillity's slightly amateurish gentlemen and ladies but the ordinary men and women doing the fighting or working, hard, in the factories. The movie *In Which we Serve*, made about a ship and its crew in 1942, featured an aristocratic captain based on Louis Mountbatten, but all the other protagonists, such as Ordinary Seaman 'Shorty' Blake, were from other ranks. There was not a middle-ranking gent in sight. The Programme's Villains, apart from Hitler and his gang, were 'spivs', who played the situation for personal profit, and the old appeasers, the latter ripped to shreds in *Guilty Men*. This book was classic Triumphalism, as was a campaign led by Lord Beaverbrook to requisition the ornamental gates presented to the old ironmaster, Baldwin, on his retirement, and have them melted down for the war effort.

The Programme's Crowning Glory? That has to be VE day.

The Programme, now in its Pomp, had a number of remarkable Big Wins. Attlee's own personal favourite was the National Insurance Act of 1946, under which everyone was guaranteed unemployment- and sickness benefits and an old-age pension, in return for paying a weekly 'stamp'. The same year saw the National Health Service Act, which mandated the Minister for Health, Nye Bevan, to set up the NHS. (Bevan finally achieved this in July 1948 – in the teeth of fierce opposition from the medical establishment: the Big Battle for the Programme.) 1946 also saw the New Towns Act, setting a massive, planned building programme in motion. In addition, Labour carried through its nationalization of the 'commanding heights of the economy': coal, electricity and the railways, which were all in public ownership by the end of 1947. Overseas, most of Britain's Asian Empire was dismantled.

The Programme had its First Big Failure in the winter of 1946/7. From late January to mid-March 1947 the country lay under deep snow. Power cuts were frequent, mainly due to shortages of coal. The Minister of Power, Emmanuel Shinwell, had run coal stocks down in late '46, hoping for a mild winter and not wishing to alienate those core Programme Heroes, miners, by asking them to increase production. The weather had other ideas.

Financial crises followed: in mid-1947 and September 1949. In the second of these, sterling was devalued from over $4 to $2.80. This was felt as a body-blow to national pride and identity. We'd won the War, but look what had happened to our currency… Body-blow this might have been, but the fall of the Attlee Programme was less dramatic than that of many: 'more a whimper than a bang' to quote historians Robert Crowcroft and Kevin Theakston. It was the other two, slower-acting Fates that did the real damage.

Several Slow Stranglers were at work. One was simply the age and fitness of the Programme's leaders. By 1950 they were suffering from ill health and weren't physically fit to govern. Another was a dilemma caused by events running ahead of the Programme. With the outbreak of the Korean War in June 1950, the government found itself helplessly pinned between a desire to participate and thus support both the UN (in which Attlee believed passionately) and America (which was effectively bankrolling the UK at that time), and the desperate need not to spend scarce money on what would be an expensive conflict.

For the voter, however, what Slowly Strangled 1945 Socialism was the continuation of rationing, plus the hectoring tone that went with it. Rationing lasted throughout the Programme's Pomp. Some items, like bread, were only rationed after the War. When the nation went to the polls in 1951, over six years after VE Day (rationing lasted longer after the war than during it), the following were still rationed: bacon, ham, other meat (more strictly rationed than it had been in 1945), butter, margarine, cooking fat, cheese, sugar, sweets, chocolate and tea.

And then there was the tone… At the start of 1948, a billboard went up around the country, showing Attlee and a slogan: "Let us all put into our work the spirit that has made this nation great. An all-out effort will increase our production by the 10% we need to turn the tide." John Bew points out that George Orwell's *1984* appeared soon after. Big Brother – or at least, Uncle Clem – is watching you!

However, it's important to understand that, to core supporters of the 1945 Programme, both rationing and the billboard were perfectly reasonable. If there was a shortage of food, then what food there was should be shared out equally. Wasn't rationing just another part of economic planning? And as for the tone, well, citizens had duties. Good thing to remind them of it from time to time! Both rationing and the billboard flowed naturally from the Programme and its Worldview, just as ignoring a posturing overseas dictator had been the natural thing for 'Mr Tranquillity' to have done a decade earlier. Such is the irony of Political Programmes: sticking to them brings greatness, but, in the long run, destruction as events and, with them, the Zeitgeist move on.

Beyond the party faithful, more and more voters were getting fed up with having goods rationed and being told to work harder. The Conservatives played on this in the 1950 election, and slashed Attlee's majority from 146 to 5. Women, in particular, swapped allegiance. Limping along with such a small majority was never going to be easy.

The Third Fate came into play when a Big Split opened up in the party. In April 1951, the administration proposed saving money on the booming (and ever more costly) NHS by charging for prescriptions and for dental and optical work. Nye Bevan resigned over the issue, as did a junior minister called Harold Wilson). Cue years of bickering between supporters of Bevan and those of at first Attlee and then the man who became his successor, Hugh Gaitskell.

A second election was called for the next year. In this one, the

Conservatives gained an overall majority of 17 – their First Taste of Power. Typical of supporters of a Programme that has thus been Dethroned, former Chancellor Hugh Dalton predicted that the new government would soon hit economic and social problems and be out of office again. He was, of course, wrong.

Sic transit gloria.

1945 Socialism

Crucible Group: At LSE, post-1931

Leader: Clement Attlee

Core Policies: Welfare State, nationalize key industries, full employment, dismantle the Asian Empire

Carried Forward from Past: Respect for traditional institutions (especially the monarchy)

Sacred Texts: *The Social Worker* (1920), Beveridge Report (1942), *Let us Face the Future* (1945)

Heroes: The ordinary working man

Villains: Capitalists, spivs, old aristocratic appeasers

Gaining Significant Influence: Attlee appointed party leader, 1935

First Taste of Power: Attlee enters Coalition, May 10th, 1940

Great Endorsement: 1945 election, 146 majority

Crowning Glory: VE day

Cultural Endorsement: *An Inspector Calls*

Counterblast: *Brideshead Revisited*

Big Wins: National Insurance Act, 1946; New Towns Act, 1946; creation of NHS, 1946 – 8; nationalization of coal, electricity and railways; Indian independence

Big Battle: Bevan vs. the BMA

The First Big Failure: 1946/7 power shortage

Body-blow: (?) Devaluation, Sept 18th, 1949

Slow Stranglers: Age/health of leaders; financial implications of the Korean War, continuation of rationing and the hectoring tone that went with it

Big Split: Bevanite rebellion over NHS charges

Dethronement: Conservative victory of 1951

Waterloo: Big Conservative victory of 1955

Fifties 'One Nation' Conservatism, 1951 - 1964

A number of younger Conservatives had been promoted to positions of responsibility in the Churchill/Attlee Coalition. 'Rab' Butler, then aged thirty-eight, was given a Cabinet post in 1941 and went on to create the 1944 Education Act, which provided free education for all. Harold Macmillan, author of a 1938 book called *The Middle Way* which advocated economic planning and a minimum wage, received a Cabinet post in 1942. While Conservative in asserting the existing social order and drawing their support mainly from the middle and upper classes, these rising stars on the left of the party were keen to protect the working classes against the more extreme consequences of *laissez faire* Capitalism (a system they referred to as 'devil-take-the-hindmost').

Looking back, the appointments of Butler and Macmillan can be seen as moments when Significant Influence was achieved by a still Aspirant Political Programme.

In 1947, the party published a pamphlet called *The Industrial Charter*, which suggested moving with times and accepting most of the Beveridge reforms. Macmillan, one of its authors, talked of 'the impossibility of unscrambling those scrambled eggs.' It would become a Sacred Text of the new Programme.

However, when it was debated at that year's Party Conference, the Charter proved controversial. Churchill was not impressed. Old-school Tory Sir Waldron Smithers, MP for Orpington, denounced it as 'milk and water socialism'.

It took another election and a large input of younger MPs to really get change moving. In 1950, nine of these new arrivals formed a group called 'One Nation'. This was a classic Crucible Group, meeting over dinner – no doubt at a venue that had found a way round meat rationing – and discussing their vision for what would soon become a new Political Programme. The group included Edward Heath, Iain Macleod, Angus Maude and Enoch Powell.

In the same year, the group published a pamphlet that bore its name, *One Nation*. In it, they argued that the Welfare State should be maintained but made to work more efficiently (a classic way of reframing the carrying forward of popular policies). Rather than serve everyone, the welfare system should be a safety net, providing "a minimum standard, above which people should be free to rise as far as their industry, their thrift, their ability or their genius may take them." Alongside the provision of this net, the government's job was to defend the nation, keep the currency sound and tax people as little as possible. It was not responsible for creating equality. The group would continue to issue influential pamphlets during the 1950s.

After this, the Programme won its First Taste of Power quickly, in the October 1951 election. This was a classic First Taste: very provisional. The Tories actually got fewer votes than Labour but more seats. This was partially because of constituency boundaries, some seats being more populous than others, but also because Labour had huge majorities in its stronghold seats, while the majorities in many Conservative ones (especially the newly-won ones) were small. But that was the system, and the 1945 Programme was duly dethroned.

The new Programme would go on to have its Great Endorsement at the next election, in May 1955, where it won by 60 seats. The party received 49.7% of the votes – a percentage it has never achieved again since, not even in the Thatcher years.

As they said they would, the new power-holders carried forward much of the old 1945 Socialist reforms, especially those inspired by Beveridge. Some historians argue that the new government kept so much of the old Programme that there was no real change of Political Programme at this time. They talk instead of 'Butskellism' (a made-up name from the Tory and Labour chancellors, Rab Butler and Hugh Gaitskell) and of a 'post-war consensus' that lasted from 1945 to 1979.

However, new Programmes always carry forward some aspects of the old. 1951 saw big changes in policy direction and even bigger ones of culture and attitude. I grew up during this era in a staunchly Conservative household, and the idea that 'our' party was part of any consensus with 'the other lot' would have seemed absurd.

In policy, nationalization was halted. Iron and steel companies, bar one, were put back in private hands. The market was prioritized over central planning. The ending of rationing, as soon as possible, was made a priority. There were no more billboards exhorting people to produce 10% more: in the new Programme's Britain, billboards would be for advertising washing machines or TVs. As David Willetts put it in *After the Landslide*, Labour was 'the party of planning and the producers' and the Conservatives 'the party of the free market and the consumers.'

But it was culture and mindset that was the most potent differentiator. Gone was the working man as Hero, busy at the coalface or shovelling the coal into the boiler of a locomotive. Now the narrative was about the middle-class family enjoying their head-earned leisure, sitting down to their unrationed traditional British Sunday roast – cooked, of course, by the proud wife, though the equally proud husband did the decent thing afterwards and helped with the washing up, while their son played with his Meccano and their daughter with her dolls. Citizens? We were all subjects of the King, and, after February 1952, a beautiful young Queen.

Were the workers dumped, then? No. The Conservatives have always been too astute to do that, with a long tradition, from Disraeli through Churchill's father, Lord Randolph, and Churchill himself, of 'Tory Democracy'. The working class was not encouraged to proudly contemplate its existing virtues, as it had been by Labour, but instead asked to stay patriotic and to better itself economically. The wherewithal to do the latter – new consumer goods – became more and more available as the 1950s continued. The far left saw this as pernicious *embourgeoisement*, the erosion of sacred class identity. Workers and their families, by and large, simply enjoyed the new stuff. "Most of our people have never had it so good," said the Programme's ultimate leader, Macmillan, in a speech in 1957.

He really did mean 'most' and would love to have said 'all'. He also meant 'our': like pre-war Baldwinites, Fifties Conservatives were paternalist. They believed in deference to the old order and its representatives. There was a sense that this order was something sacred, which had evolved over centuries and had made our nation great. Liberal intellectuals and socialists who criticized or mocked it were 'too clever by half'. Macmillan wrote in his diary how much he hated holidays where there were 'masses of tourists' but loved the moors where he went shooting, where 'the hills, the keepers, the farmers, the farmers' sons, the drivers… always remined the same'.

The era tuned into radio programmes like 'Two Way Family

Favourites', with Doris Day telling us in 1956 that whatever would be, would be, or (for my generation) 'Children's Favourites', with its emblematic theme tune *Puffin' Billy*. From 1955, the televised streets of Dock Green were patrolled by the avuncular PC George Dixon. In the theatre, there was the gentle humour of Flanders and Swann or Terrence Rattigan's moral dilemmas of aristocrats or the upper middle class. The standard high culture menu featured Dickens, Shakespeare and classical music (including sitting with a pained look through something, hopefully brief, by Hindemith or Stravinsky).

The War, of course, cast a long shadow over the era's culture. But it was presented in a different way. It hadn't been won by Shorty Blake after all, but by daring young bucks, often played by Kenneth More. This Programme's war heroes were dashing and, after all, gentlemanly.

There was a flip side to all this apparent lightness: an insistence on conformity. A certain amount of youthful exuberance was fine, especially for chaps, but there were boundaries. If you found yourself outside these, you were in trouble.

The Villains of the Fifties Conservative culture were 'the Russians' and bolshy trade unionists intent on perpetuating a now-outdated class war. But the Villain-making also seeped into the (by many people) strongly-held prejudices of the era, particularly homophobia.

Homophobia was linked to worries about security, as it was felt that gay men, in particular, could be targets for blackmail. (The idea that you could change this by simply accepting gay people didn't occur to Fifties Conservatives.) But there was something more visceral to the prejudice than this. The Fifties seem to be an era of particularly virulent homophobia. The most notable victim was Alan Turing, but many other people suffered. At the end of 1954, there were over 1000 men in prison for committing homosexual acts. A number of them had been caught in entrapment exercises set up by the police. In the same year, the Home Secretary, David Maxwell-Fyfe, who once described homosexuality as a 'plague', ordered an official report on the issue. One must assume that he hoped it would advocate taking a firmer line, but when the Wolfenden Report came out, in 1957, it favoured liberalization. Maxwell-Fyfe, by then in the Lords, voted against it. The recommendations weren't implemented.

Racial prejudice was also a feature of 1950s life, occasionally erupting into violence, but the Programme didn't play that card, unlike their active homophobia (and unlike some Conservatives in the 1960s). However, they did quietly allow a 'colour bar', whereby non-whites could not get any kind of supervisory position, to exist in many workplaces. The one at Euston station was not ended until 1966.

The Programme's insistence on uniformity spilled over into censorship, which was tightened in the early 1950s. In 1954, Donald McGill's saucy seaside postcards were banned from a number of resorts. Magistrates in Swindon ordered the destruction of a translation of Boccaccio's *Decameron* in a local bookshop. Later on, in 1960, the establishment would attempt to prevent publication of DH Lawrence's erotic novella *Lady Chatterley's Lover*, which, according to the leading barrister for the Crown, was not something you would wish 'your wife or your servants' to read.

There was, of course, a Counterblast. In 1956, John Osborne's *Look Back in Anger* premiered at the Royal Court Theatre in May 1956, its young hero furious about the class system and what he sees as the stifling smugness of the era. The Angry Young Men had arrived.

However, many more young men – and women – were having fun rather than getting angry. Top of the UK charts in November 1955 was *Rock Around the Clock* by Bill Haley and His Comets. In 1957, Elvis Presley (or his music, anyway) really hit the UK, with his first UK Number One, *All Shook Up*. Rock'n'roll wasn't so much a Counterblast to Fifties Conservatism as a message from an alternative universe that completely ignored it. The new popular culture faltered after Elvis was drafted into the US Army, but would come back, even more vibrant, later, ready to chime with the Programme's successor and be skilfully corralled into the political arena by it.

The Programme's Great Escape was the Suez Crisis of 1956. Egyptian President Gamal Abdel Nasser nationalized the strategically essential canal. Britain and another nation smarting from diminution of Empire, France, decided to grab it back (with some help from Israel) by military force. Their operation began successfully, but the rest of the world rounded on them and they were forced to abandon it.

This was a national humiliation. However, the Programme did not collapse after it, despite talk to that effect around the time. Many old-school patriot voters had supported the action. When a *post mortem* debate on Suez was conducted in parliament in 1957, the government had a big enough majority to survive, despite a few defections. Radical opponents crowed at the establishment's embarrassment and fumed at the result of the parliamentary debate; a few careers (including that of PM Anthony Eden) suffered, but otherwise little changed.

In fact, the Programme gained momentum. Eden was replaced by a more effective leader, Harold Macmillan, who would keep the job for nearly seven years, and the period has gone down in history as 'the Macmillan era'. With its proper Leader now in place, the Programme had a long Pomp. That is not to say it had everything easy: the era saw the height of the Cold War (or one height of it, anyway), with the Berlin Wall and Cuba crises of 1961/2. But Macmillan played his diplomatic cards skilfully, and ended up a co-signatory to a treaty banning the testing of the nuclear weapons that had, at one point, seemed to threaten the entire life of the planet.

Macmillan dealt well with his mercurial adversary in the Kremlin, Nikita Khrushchev: his foreign policy nemesis was much closer to home, just across the English Channel. Having fought in one European war and observed another, Macmillan was determined to get Britain into what was then called the EEC, the European club of France, Germany, Benelux and Italy. Long negotiations were carried out – but in the end, these all hit the brick wall of General de Gaulle.

The General's "Non!", announced at a press conference in January 1963, was a public relations disaster for the Macmillan administration. This was its First Big Failure. As it was essentially foreign policy, it did not hurt British citizens directly. But rejection dented the confidence of the administration badly.

The Body-blow came shortly afterwards, as the Profumo Affair unfolded over 1963. John Profumo, a minister, had an affair with Christine Keeler, a young girl-about-town whose other lovers included a Russian spy. This, in itself, appalled more strait-laced party supporters (including Macmillan). But Profumo then lied about it in the House of Commons, threatening libel suits for anyone who raised the issue again, before finally admitting the truth.

The Fifties Conservative Programme had been built on the belief that the old class system worked. The people at the top might have privilege, but they strove for the common good and kept to the same personal rules as everyone else. The Profumo Affair gave the lie to this. It was part of a rival narrative, a Slow Strangler for the Programme, that the class system was holding the country back.

Allied to this was a growing awareness of Britain's economic underperformance relative to other European countries. Germany was booming – according to some economists, its GDP had actually overtaken ours in the middle of the 1950s. France and Italy were growing faster than us, too. 'National Productivity Year', launched in November 1962, did little to change this – a set of stamps issued to celebrate the campaign became notorious for printing errors.

Macmillan's health declined sharply after the Profumo affair and forced him to retire on the eve of that year's Party Conference in October. Who should the Conservatives get to replace him? Someone in tune with the new mood, obviously. Someone young, like America's dynamic new president, John F Kennedy. Someone upwardly mobile.

The party grandees chose the sixty-year-old 14th Earl of Home, a man so patrician that you had to come from the right side of the tracks to know how to pronounce his name properly (one said "Hume").

Despite this, and an admission that he 'did his economics with matchsticks', Home was not the upper-class twit that his detractors gleefully presented him as. He was intelligent, likeable and conscientious. But his selection sent out totally the wrong message to a country eager for change. The old Programme was now Degenerating, and would soon be put out of its misery.

Fifties 'One Nation' Conservatism

Leader (eventually): Harold Macmillan

Core Policies: Mixed economy

Carried forward: Beveridge 'safety net'

Crucible Group: 'One Nation' dining club

Sacred Texts: *The Middle Way* (1938), *The Industrial Charter* (1947), *One Nation* (1950)

Heroes: The middle-class family

Villains: The Russians, old-fashioned class warriors, (for some) homosexuals

Gaining Significant Influence: Butler and Macmillan join wartime Cabinet

First Taste of Power: Narrow victory of 1951

Great Endorsement: 60-seat victory in 1955

Crowning Glory: Coronation / Ascent of Everest

Cultural Endorsement: *'Que sera, sera', Dixon of Dock Green,* Flanders and Swann, the plays of Terrence Rattigan

Cultural Counterblast: *Look Back in Anger*

Big Wins: Removal of rationing, test ban treaty

Great Escape: Suez Crisis

First Big Failure: Rejected application to join EEC

Body-blow: Profumo Affair

Slow Stranglers: Poor economic performance relative to Europe, public loss of faith in the old class system

Dethronement: Labour victory of 1964

Waterloo: Labour victory of 1966

'White Heat' Modernization, 1964 - 1970

A radically different Programme was waiting in the wings. As usual, it first got its First Taste of Power, winning the 1964 election, by a tiny majority: 4. But that was enough.

The Big New Idea of the Programme was modernization. Its Leader was Harold Wilson (though its lasting achievements would turn out to be those of his Foil, Roy Jenkins, Home Secretary from 1965 to 1967).

Wilson is often presented as an opportunist. Though he could be one at times, he was much a more serious thinker than that. He moved on from participating in internal party squabbles to creating a Big New Idea, with clear, fresh set of Values and clear, fresh Stories. Wilson wasn't just 'a Bevanite' or 'a Gaitskellite'; he was the creator of a new Political Programme.

The son of an industrial chemist, he believed passionately in technology, planning, and the ability of these to change society. These ideas were nurtured in a Crucible Group which met at the Reform Club in the 1950s. It was led by left-leaning Nobel Prize winning physicist Patrick Blackett, and included leading scientists and writers – and some Labour politicians, especially Wilson.

Wilson didn't create his Big New Idea because he spotted a gap in the political marketplace, he did so because he believed in it.

The new ideas were set out in a policy document that can be seen as the Sacred Text of Wilsonism, *Signposts for the Sixties*, which he coauthored in 1960. But the new Worldview was most forcefully expressed in Wilson's Party Conference speech at Scarborough in 1963, when he inspired his audience with his vision of a technology-driven society. There would be 'planning on an unprecedented scale to meet automation without unemployment; a pooling of talent in which all classes could compete and prosper; a vast extension of state-sponsored research; a completely new concept of education; an alliance of science and socialism.' A new Britain was going to be 'forged' in the 'white heat' of this revolution.

The people doing this forging would be very different from the Heroes of the old Programme: the old, languid, educated-in-Classics-at-public-school, southern, C of E Fifties Conservatives. Wilson was a generation younger than Macmillan, and grammar-school educated. His background was Northern and Nonconformist. He was hard-working, a meritocrat (in the non-ironic sense of the word).

There was a huge Cultural Endorsement. Over 80% of UK households now owned TV sets, and viewers could watch the biting satire of programmes like *That Was The Week That Was*, or the street realism of *Z Cars*, a police series that depicted realistic Liverpudlian policemen in their shiny new Ford Zephyrs. *The Wednesday Play*, which ran for the whole time of the Programme, looked critically at social issues, and featured top-quality works like *Cathy Come Home*, *Up the Junction* and Denis Potter's *Nigel Barton* miniseries.

And then there were The Beatles… Wilson was not a fan – he much preferred Gilbert and Sullivan – but he knew how to harness their popularity. The Fab Four were misfits in the old order but godsends to the new one. They were working class (ish), but had no intention of being defined by their roots (Lennon's *Working Class Hero* wasn't written until 1970). Instead, they became something class-transcendent, superstars, and created the music by which the people set free by the new Programme celebrated their lives. They also enjoyed a good laugh at the new Villains, the supporters of the old Programme – watch the train sequence in the film *A Hard Day's Night*.

A second election, in March 1966, gave the Programme its Great Endorsement, 98 seats worth. This was followed, on 30th July, by its Crowning Glory (south of Hadrian's Wall and east of Offa's Dyke, anyway), when England won the football World Cup.

However, beneath these appearances, trouble was already brewing. Wilson's planned economic changes were not as effective as had been hoped. He had created a new Department of Economic Affairs in 1964. This was supposed to be a rival to the economically cautious Treasury: its brief was bold economic planning. However, from the start, reality kept on refusing to fit in with the DEA's plans.

Two particularly pesky refuseniks were international currency traders (demonized in the Programme's mythology as 'the gnomes of Zurich') and the domestic trade unions. A strong pound was part of the plan (it also signalled national pride and confidence). But Britain was importing more than it was exporting, which put the pound under perpetual pressure. A strike in 1966 by the National Union of Seamen, who wanted a bigger pay rise than the planners allowed, intensified this. Money was required to prop up the currency, so cuts had to be made elsewhere.

Wilson found himself caught between two options: formally devalue the pound, or make spending cuts that would effectively mean the end of the grand economic plan. Historians now all seem to agree that he should have taken the former route. Spooked by memories of 1949, he took the latter.

In terms of the model proposed in this book, this meant a U-turn, diverging from the Core Policies of his Programme, which were designed to build a rationally-planned, technology-driven economy, initially supported by government expenditure.

Luckily for the Programme, it had another aspect to its Big New Idea. If Wilson wanted to modernize the economy, his Foil, Roy Jenkins, wanted to modernize our values and lifestyles. When Jenkins became Home Secretary, he was the youngest person to hold the job since Winston Churchill back in 1910. It showed. The Beatles, who never wrote any songs about five-year plans or Magnox reactors, were much better allies for him than for Wilson. Both Jenkins and John Lennon understood the deep need for the freedom to express oneself by living an intense cultural and emotional life. (Jenkins was hardly a fan, however. There are no swinging sixties tracks in the music he later chose for Desert Island Discs, where the only modern piece is Vangelis' *Chariots of Fire*.)

Jenkins' part of the Programme had been trailed in two Sacred Texts. Anthony Crosland's *The Future of Socialism* was published in 1956. Crosland, a *bon viveur*, wanted above all for everyone to have the same opportunities for good living as he had. Criticizing the rather drab world of Attleean citizenship, he wanted Britain to be 'a more colourful and civilized country to live in'.

In 1959, Jenkins published his own book, *The Labour Case*. He wrote: 'Let us be on the side of those who want people to be free to live their own lives, to make their own mistakes, and to decide, in an adult way and provided they do not infringe the rights of others, the code by which they wish to live; and on the side of experiment and brightness, of better buildings and better food, of better music (jazz as well as Bach) and better books, of fuller lives and greater freedom. In the long run these things will be more important than the most perfect of economic policies.'

In Jenkins' two years as Home Secretary in this Programme, bills were passed to legalize abortion, decriminalize homosexual acts, simplify the painful divorce system and abolish birching in prisons. He also initiated bills that ended up being passed once he had left the Home Office, removing the antiquated theatre censorship system and outlawing the refusal of housing, employment or public services to someone on grounds of race. Subsequent Political Programmes have grumbled at Jenkins' reforms. Thatcherites loathed them, and even Tony Blair enjoyed the odd pop at them. No subsequent Programme has undone any of them, however, and they have become part of modern British life.

Home Secretary Jenkins was also a Wilsonian modernizer of the police, cutting the number of forces drastically, and of the court system, introducing majority verdicts in for a range of offences. Both reforms were initially resisted by the bodies in question, but have subsequently been accepted as constructive and necessary.

Jenkins' Britain became a place of cultural celebration, driven by young people, many from working class origins. The Beatles were the flagship, but there were a hundred other great bands and artists, such as musician Ray Davies (son of a slaughterhouse worker), photographer Terry O'Neill (born in Romford)(he became famous for taking a picture of the old Programme's RA Butler asleep at Heathrow Airport) and fashion designer Mary Quant, from a Welsh mining family. *The Liverpool Scene,* a 1967 anthology featuring young Merseyside poets, was tutted at by the establishment – 'popsters and barbarians' said one critic – but sold half a million copies.

Indian and Chinese restaurants appeared on the streets of British towns and cities. Package holidays to sunnier climes became available, especially thanks to the Thomson Organization, which entered that market in 1965. The contraceptive pill was made available to unmarried women in 1967, the same year of the first colour TV broadcast (of Wimbledon on BBC2). BBC1 and ITV went colour in 1969.

If there was a Counterblast to the new culture, it was muted. Christopher Booker's *The Neophiliacs* critiqued it in 1969, but few people were listening. If there was a lively cultural alternative to Swinging London, it lay in the even more swinging 'alternative society' of drugs, ultra-left/anarchist protest and sexual experimentation, which stuck two, probably stoned, fingers up to parliamentary politics of any kind. The 'alternatives' excoriated Wilson for supporting US involvement in Vietnam – unfairly. Wilson, an Atlanticist at heart, risked alienating his most important global ally by keeping the UK out of the conflict, something that the more hip, liberal Tony Blair proved unable to do forty years later.

Meanwhile, Wilson's half of the Programme spluttered along, bedevilled by constant sterling crises. Following the 1966 one, another followed in 1967, also triggered by a strike, this time in the docks. This second crisis forced Wilson's hand: the pound had to be devalued after all. It wasn't as spectacular as 1949, but the cut from the pound's being worth $2.80 to $2.40 was still seen as humiliating. Nobody was impressed by a speech where he told voters that 'the pound in your pocket has not been devalued'. The gnomes had won.

Wilson tried to keep his White Heat revolution going, but to little effect. Mergers between large companies, especially in the automotive, electrical and computing sectors, were encouraged by a new Industrial Reorganization Corporation. The hope was that these would create greater efficiency. The record was patchy, the mergers working sometimes but often creating culture clashes between participants. A Selective Employment Tax tried to boost employment in export-based manufacturing and take it away from domestic services. It did little to boost manufacturing and damaged the service sector. In many British towns, Wilsonite planning saw modern rectangular concrete office- or 'tower' accommodation blocks replacing older buildings. Some of those older buildings, no doubt, had been in need of renovation, but they had created community. Their replacements were bland and, after the partial collapse of Ronan Point in 1968, not considered fully safe.

The once-mighty flagship Department of Economic Affairs was not delivering the goods, either. It was wound up in 1969, the Treasury quietly rubbing its hands and taking back what was left of its role. The DEA lives on as the 'Department of Administrative Affairs' in the TV sitcom *Yes Minister*.

Wilson's Big New Idea of putting technology centre stage had seemed timely and relevant. Yet its Pomp was short-lived. The Programme seemed to have difficulty choosing the right Normal Politics to go with its powerful, liberating vision. Economic planning turned out to be tricky. Its failure led to a scepticism about governmental planning that has lasted to this day. Whether that is justified is open to question. Is planning a bad idea, end of story, or did Wilson and the DEA just go about it the wrong way?

Still, Wilsonism did have Big Wins. Higher education was expanded. A lasting legacy of White Heat modernization is the Open University, established in 1969. This aimed to improve the national level of education, offering degree courses to people who, having missed the academic boat as youngsters, wanted to climb on board later in life. This is still going strong.

The motorway network was developed and driving made much safer thanks to the 70mph speed limit, the introduction of the breathalyser and rules on seatbelts. This represented a major opening up of life for millions of people from Wilson's own background who suddenly found that they could afford cars. Both the new roads and the new rules were an essential part of this. For Fifties Conservatives, 'motoring' had been for the few, and tiresome rules were seen as unnecessary. As the roads expanded and filled up with the 'many', rules became necessary.

Housing was improved in a number of ways, with over a million new homes built, the expansion of New Towns, legislation to protect tenants against unscrupulous landlords and a scheme to help poorer people get on the property ladder.

The Wilson cabinet also featured many more women than any previous one. If the classic Great Offices of State were still held by men, the female voice was influential. Many of the transport reforms were driven by Barbara Castle. Jennie Lee was put in charge of the Open University project, one dear to Wilson's heart. (Castle was made 'First Secretary of State', a rather nebulous title similar to Deputy PM.)

The Programme soon found its Slow Strangler, or rather two of them: the global currency markets and deteriorating industrial relations. The second of these grew ever more destructive as the sixties drew to a close, with unofficial, 'wildcat' strikes adding to the existing unwillingness of the unions to go along with the planners. During most of the decade, the number of working days lost due to strikes was under 4 million a year. In 1968, it was 4.7 million, and in 1969, it was 6.8 million.

In response to this, Labour produced a white paper called *In Place of Strife*. This proposed a number of measures, including the insistence on a ballot of all members if a union in a key industry called a strike, a 28-day cooling off period for wildcat strikes, and stiff penalties for any union that broke the new rules. The cabinet was divided over it, and it never made it onto the statute book.

The result of all this was a slow ratcheting up of inflation, which passed 5% in 1969. Given the rates that would soon prevail, this sounds peanuts – but at the time it looked scary, not having been that high since 1952.

Nevertheless, there was real growth in the economy. Wilson, with the backing of his cabinet, called an early election. Arguably one reason for the timing was the 1970 football World Cup, for which England were favourites. The date chosen, June 18th, was just after the semi-finals. Memo to politicians: Crowning Glories happen naturally or not at all. England never reached the semis. 2-0 up in our quarter final against Germany at one point, we ended up losing 3-2.

The Conservative leader Ted Heath came up with a catchy Slogan, claiming he would cut prices 'at a stroke' (exactly how was never made clear, but such is the way of Slogans). Regrettably, another factor in the victory was probably the playing of the race card by certain Conservative politicians, though Heath, a fundamentally decent man, did not approve. Heath won by a majority of 30. Programme over.

After its defeat, White Heat kept cooling down. Technology stopped being sexy and started appearing as a Villain. Even back in 1963, when Wilson gave his famous speech, the long-term damage caused to the planet by the unthinking use of technology was already being flagged up by Rachel Carson's ground-breaking *Silent Spring*. In Britain, the 1967 wrecked tanker *Torrey Canyon* spilled millions of gallons of crude oil onto once-beautiful Cornish beaches, shocking many of us – especially once pictures of seabirds coated in oil appeared in the press. By 1972, the Club of Rome (nothing to do with the EU and its Treaty of Rome) was talking of 'natural limits to growth'. EF Schumacher proclaimed that small was beautiful in 1973. The rising counter-culture of the era had its own Worldview, of nature as a source of beauty and spiritual strength, in need of defence against uptight, over-rational, arrogant men who sought to exploit and ruin it for selfish, short-term, material ends.

The 1973/4 oil crisis bought this message crashing home. Our wealth-creating heavy-industrial technology was not only morally questionable in the eyes of some people, but was in practice unsustainable, as it was based on flimsy premises: boundless cheap oil and a myth that both production and consumption were free of negative externalities (cases where the costs of economic activity get secretly shunted onto someone else – or, as in the case of much environmental damage, onto the planet and its future).

'White Heat' Modernization

Leader: Harold Wilson
Foil: Roy Jenkins
Core Policies: Planned economy. Social liberalization
Crucible Group: Patrick Blackett's Reform Club group
Sacred Texts: *The Labour Case* (1959). *Signposts to the Sixties* (1960)
Hero: Ex-grammar-school scientist/planner in white coat
Villains: Privileged elite, 'old boy network', 'gnomes of Zurich'
Gaining Significant Influence: Wilson becomes Party Leader, 1963
First Taste of Power: Narrow victory of 1964
Great Endorsement: Big victory in 1966
Crowning Glory: England win World Cup, 30th June 1966
Cultural Endorsements: *Z-Cars,* The Wednesday Play, The Beatles (and many other bands), 'Swinging London'
Cultural Counterblast: The full-on alternative society
Big Wins: Jenkins' social reforms, creation of Open University
First Big Failure: Devaluation of the pound, 1967
Body-blow: Failure of *In Place of Strife* white paper
Slow Stranglers: Currency markets, industrial unrest and inflation
Dethronement: Conservative victory of 1970
Waterloo: Oil crisis of 1973/4

The 1970s: Two Aspirant Programmes that never made it

1. Heathism

The Conservative Party had ditched Alec Douglas-Home in 1965 and appointed in his stead a Harold Wilson lookalike: grammar-school alumnus and meritocrat Ted Heath. Heath, an original member of the One Nation group back in 1950, didn't set up a Crucible Group, but did the next best thing: organize a conference to thrash out a new Action Plan for the party. This took place at the Selsdon Park Hotel, a former Victorian country house in what was by then leafy suburbia, in January 1970.

At this, Heath appeared to ditch his old one-nation caution and presided over a conference that looked to the economic right for inspiration. Less state expenditure. No more support for ailing businesses ('lame ducks') or meddling with business ownership *à la* Industrial Reorganization Corporation. No planned levels of prices and incomes. No Keynesian macroeconomic tinkering. The market would be in charge.

Wilson was dismissive, talking of 'Selsdon Man' as if the conference were a gathering of vicious prehistoric anthropoids (in fact, the delegates were ahead of their time). But Heath's party won the election that followed that summer. Its 30-seat majority was not a Great Endorsement, but it was a decent First Taste of Power for the new Aspirant Programme.

As with all Democratic Revolutions, some of the old Programme was carried forward into the new. There was a Wilsonian technocratic feel to Heathism. Efficiency remained a watchword. Some old counties were replaced by efficient (in theory) new ones. The old currency of pounds, shillings and pence was decimalized (a Labour policy, but it could have been cancelled).

However, the new Programme soon got into trouble. The Selsdon agenda proved impossible to realize. In 1971, the government bailed out Rolls Royce, which had encountered cost overruns on its new RB211 aero engine. This was a wise move, as the engine would go on to be a huge success, but it was a major U-turn. In the same year, Upper Clyde Shipbuilders went bankrupt. The government refused to bail it out – and its shop stewards organized a 'work-in'. Cue another U-turn, as the embarrassed government finally stepped in after all.

Meanwhile, unemployment had begun to rise. Heath's new Chancellor, Anthony Barber, tried to counteract this with classic Keynesian methods, reflating the economy in a 'Dash for Growth'. Yet another big U-turn.

As a result of this, inflation, which had dipped during 1971/2, giving the illusion that it was back under control, began to rise again – and this time it kept rising. So much for 'at a stroke'. Unions began competing in a game of 'ask for the biggest pay rise'. This resulted in yet another U-turn, the creation of a Prices and Incomes policy, which the unions simply ignored.

All hell broke loose, with inflation soaring, strikes hitting levels not seen since 1926 and, ultimately, industry being forced to work a three-day week. The UK stock market crash of 1973/4 was worse than anything from the 1930s, with the index losing an astonishing 73% of its value.

One can argue that circumstances were against Heath. He was unlucky in a personal way. His most able supporter, his Chancellor Ian Macleod, died a few weeks after the victory. Macleod would have been less likely to launch Barber's disastrous Dash for Growth. He was unlucky geopolitically, too. The 1973/4 oil crisis occurred on his watch. In a deeper way, he was unlucky because the time simply wasn't right for him. The nation had to go through more pain before enough people realized that trade unions, while an essential part of a decent democracy, aren't supposed to run the country.

However, from the perspective presented in this book, Heath also made big mistakes. He came up with an Aspirant Programme, convinced the electorate of it, then dumped a large chunk of it. He was a fair-weather Selsdonian, but Political Programme Leaders cannot be 'fair-weather'. Whatever the rights and wrongs of their Programme, once they have placed themselves at the head of it, they must remain loyal to its Worldview and Core Policies. The Enoch Powell quote I mentioned earlier, about the dangers of 'seeking to govern in direct opposition to the principles with which [an administration has been] entrusted with the right to govern', dates from this time.

However, there was another aspect to 'Heathism', and here Heath stuck to his guns and the Programme succeeded. Heath believed passionately that Britain should join the European Communities (a.k.a. the 'Common Market'). It was part of the 1970 manifesto, and on 1st January, 1973, the UK, along with Denmark and Ireland, joined. A Big Win.

However, too many Core Policies had been ditched. In the face of a miners' strike in February 1974, Heath called an election on the simple question: 'Who governs Britain?' 'Not you,' the electorate replied, though it couldn't really decide who did. No party emerged with an overall majority, though Harold Wilson had four more seats than Heath. After a few days trying to form alliances with smaller parties, Heath quit Number Ten. His Programme never got a Great Endorsement.

Heathism: Selsdon and Europe

Leader: Ted Heath
Carried forward: Meritocracy, focus on efficiency
Gaining Significant Influence: Heath becomes Party Leader in 1965
Crucible Group: Conference at Selsdon Park Hotel
First Taste of Power: Election victory of 1970
Great Endorsement: *not achieved*
Big Win: Joining EC in 1973
First Big Failure: Series of U-turns
Body-blow: Three-day week
Slow Stranglers: Deteriorating industrial relations, relentless fall of stock market
Dethronement: Labour election victory of 1974

2. The Social Contract

A Labour government took power instead. Harold Wilson was still party Leader, but this was Wilson Mark 2. The events and mood-change of the early 1970s had destroyed the appeal of White Heat. Instead, the new Aspirant Political Programme had a Big New Idea, the Social Contract. This was essentially a deal between the Labour Party and the unions. Labour would put in place a set of policies of which the unions approved, and in return the unions would moderate their pay demands.

Neither side really kept to the bargain. One can have a playground argument about who started it, but it seems more sensible to say that the idea was doomed from the start. I suspect that the larger union leaders meant to keep to it, but they proved incapable of controlling their more militant shop-stewards. The government didn't help by cutting public expenditure – a U-turn, though arguably unavoidable given the state of the economy, which soon became so parlous that we had to borrow money from the IMF.

Wilson retired in 1976, shortly after his 60th birthday. He was replaced by Jim Callaghan, a classic Replacement Leader, solid and decent but not driven to power on the crest of the Zeitgeist, the way full-on Political Programme Leaders are. In 1977, the Gallup polling organization asked Britons who they thought was the most powerful man in the country. The answer was not Callaghan but Jack Jones, General Secretary of the Transport and General Workers' Union.

The Social Contract finally imploded in the 'Winter of Discontent' in 1978/1979. There were strikes by lorry drivers, railwaymen, NHS workers, refuse collectors and, most emblematic, gravediggers. Many of these strikes were wildcat, called on the whim of an individual shop steward eager to carve out a reputation for militancy. Britain being Britain, the weather also took a hand, with a vicious cold spell.

My left-wing friends insist much of that narrative was a product of right-wing media, but I remember walking through Central London with stinking streets full of rubbish piled up in corners, and sensing that things had got terminally out of hand. Maybe our nose is our most sensitive political organ.

Labour's attempt at a 1970s Political Programme ended up a failure, and resulted in their being voted out of office on May 3rd, 1979. The party immediately proceeded to dissolve into warring factions, without even waiting for a true Great Endorsement for their rivals. The 1980 Labour Party Conference was a particularly vicious affair. Callaghan resigned as leader soon after and was replaced by Michael Foot, an old trooper of the left who had been one of the authors of *Guilty Men* back in 1940. Groups like the Trotskyite Militant Tendency began to call for ever more power to be given to party activists. In 1981, the 'Gang of Four' – which included Roy Jenkins – split from Labour and founded the Social Democratic Party.

> ## The Social Contract
>
> Leader: Harold Wilson (Mark 2)
> Replacement Leader: Jim Callaghan
> Carried forward: Attempts at Prices and Incomes policies
> First Taste of Power: Largest party after election of 1974
> Great Endorsement: *not achieved*
> First Big Failure: Cash handout from International Monetary Fund, 1977
> Body-blow: Winter of Discontent, 1978/9
> Slow Strangler: Industrial relations
> Dethronement: Conservative victory of 1979
> Waterloo: 1980 Labour Party Conference

So that was the 1970s, a strange decade when both parties attempted to launch Political Programmes but neither succeeded, both getting one hand on power but neither receiving the giant 'Yes!' from the voting public that gives a Programme the confidence and time to put its Action Plan into practice, safe in the knowledge of a thumping majority.

Was this due to inept leadership? Maybe a bit, but at a deeper level, there was something unusually febrile about that decade. It really did seem that 'the system' was breaking down. My own belief is that it looked that way because it was true – from late 1973, anyway. The middle years of the decade signalled the end of an era of industrial production and mass consumption based not just on cheap oil but, more lasting, on the belief that the planet could take all the negative externalities we chose to throw at it.

Underlying all the post-war Political Programmes had been a sense that we had a machine chugging nicely along, which generated perpetually increasing wealth. Attlee, Macmillan and Wilson led debates about who should own that machine, how its output should be divided, and how to fine-tune it so it worked best. During the 1970s, a scary thought arose: supposing this machine had a limited life-span and we were reaching the end of that? Supposing, as a popular phrase of the time had it, there were 'no more goodies in the pipeline'?

Frightening, indeed.

The popular culture of the era became tinged with doubt. Hollywood caught a severe case of paranoia, with movies like *The Parallax View* and *The Conversation* (both from 1974) or *Taxi Driver* (1976). It took *Star Wars* (1977) to get the mood simple and upbeat again. British music raged with punk, or looked darkly inward via albums like Pink Floyd's *The Wall* (1979). Of course, there was still plenty of fun to be had, bopping to Glam Rock or disco, but the fraying at the edges was noticeable.

With the new decade, however, something changed. Not just the arrival of a party with a genuine Political Programme, but, behind that, a new element to the wealth-generating process that didn't deplete irreplaceable resources or spew out pollution. This was Information Technology. Computers had been used before 1980: huge rooms full of them, issuing endless reams of lined green paper. As the new decade advanced, they became ever more compact, powerful, cheaper, more user-friendly and more useful to organizations of all kinds, in all sorts of novel ways. Whole new industries came into being.

This did not mean that the economy suddenly stopped pouring rubbish into the environment, but it did mean that it was less profoundly reliant on so doing. 1973 was the year that Britain chucked the most CO2 into the atmosphere, 660,000 kilotons of the stuff. We are now emitting around 350,000 kilotons, and all major political parties want to bring that down to 0.

Sadly for the planet, this trend has only been visible in the UK and mainland Europe. The USA, Canada and Australia all emit more CO2 than they did in 1973, and the developing countries put out massively more. China, which emitted around 970,000 kilotons in 1973, now produces over 10,000,000 annually.

As the 1980s unfolded, with the new technological model developing and a new wealth-creating machine getting into gear, politicians could get back to debating ownership, fair shares and optimization, which is what happened before the 1970s and is what has happened since – though we may soon be in for another existential crisis.

The implication of this is that there are technological/economic 'eras' that last much, much longer than any Political Programme. This does not invalidate the Political Programme/Democratic Revolution model. Unless you're Karl Marx, you can have one underlying dominant nexus of technologies and several radically different ways of structuring and organizing society around that nexus. The former will clearly influence the latter, but it does not determine the choice of them.

Thatcherism, 1979 - 1997

The Worldview of the Thatcherite Political Programme has deep roots in the past – like 1945 Socialism, the Canon can be seen as vast. Arguably the first inspiration was Adam Smith, back in 1776 (or at least Smith when he talked about a 'hidden hand' guiding the economy and wrote, "It is not through the benevolence of the butcher, the brewer or the baker that we expect our dinner, but from their regard to their own interest.") A much later addition to the Canon was the work of FA von Hayek, especially *The Road to Serfdom* – a book that Churchill had cited in 1945, but which had then been dropped by One Nation Conservatives as too radical – and *The Constitution of Liberty*. Another sacred text was Milton Friedman's 1962 *Capitalism and Freedom*.

These books highlighted the centrality of the market to the economy. The market was, they argued, an amazing machine for sending constantly updated signals to producers, workers and consumers about what they should or should not produce, charge for their labour and buy. From those decisions, resources would be allocated in a way that was infinitely more efficient than anything a worthy Wilsonian planner could come up with.

Hayek argued also argued that planners were busybodies. For him, the free market was a guarantor of political freedom – the polar opposite of Marxian claims that Capitalism enslaved the individual.

On a less highbrow level, Margaret Thatcher carried the *Ten Cannots* of William C H Boetcker (often misattributed to Abraham Lincoln) in her iconic handbag.

All these ideas were nurtured and turned into policy options in various 'think tanks'. The Institute for Economic Affairs (IEA) was founded in 1955 by Anthony Fisher, who made his fortune from factory farming. After Ted Heath's U-turns, a group of market-minded Tory MPs founded the Selsdon Group, dedicated to carrying on the now-abandoned policies of the 1970 election-winner. However, the most significant of these bodies, the true Crucible Group of Thatcherism, was the Centre for Policy Studies, founded in 1974 by Keith Joseph, Alfred Sherman and Margaret Thatcher herself.

In the following year, Thatcher was elected the party's leader, replacing Heath: the Programme's accession to Significant Influence.

She became Prime Minister in the election of May 1979. Her majority was decent – 43 seats – but she still had an enormous amount of work to do, convincing many of her colleagues (let alone the country) of her radical new Programme. A less firm hand could easily have been shaken off the tiller: this was a First Taste of Power, a trial run, not a great roar of public approval.

The economy plunged into recession, but Thatcher refused to use the traditional Keynesian lever of boosting demand by pumping money into it, arguing that this would reignite inflation. Instead, she sought to free up the 'supply' side, trying to make it easier for businesses to create jobs and wealth.

The recession continued. Party grandees told her she should do a U-turn, but she replied with her 'the lady's not for turning' speech at the 1980 Party Conference at Brighton. In March 1981, 364 leading economists wrote her an open letter via the Times newspaper, criticizing her policies – a classic 'shocked old guard' response of horror. "You can't do that!"

She ignored them. That is what Political Programme Leaders do.

Many old manufacturing companies went to the wall, but inflation fell, and the economy began to recover, albeit slowly and painfully.

Labour helped her in the polls with its lurch to the left, but soon neither party was faring well. Would the new Alliance break through, prove to be the real Political Programme for the 1980s, and render Thatcherism another Aspirant that never quite made it?

The Falklands War settled that debate. My own personal view is that Thatcher would have seen off the Alliance anyway, as the Zeitgeist was heading in her direction. The Alliance was, in many ways, reheated seventies 'Social Contract' Labour, and the nation wanted more radical change. But I can't prove that (any more than people with the opposing view can prove theirs).

Some conspiracy theorists say that Thatcher set the war up, feigning weakness before it to confuse the macho Argentinian generals. Like most conspiracy theories, this doesn't fit the facts. Thatcher tried to negotiate, via her Foreign Secretary Francis Pym, but was rebuffed. She went to war because she felt she had to defend (very) British citizens against a foreign dictatorship.

She took a genuine risk in doing so. The British force was 8,000 miles from home. It was outnumbered. It did not have air superiority. Britain won due to the outstanding qualities of its servicemen and to slices of luck – a number of bombs that hit British ships failed to detonate. So, yes, Britain gained the victory, and the celebration of that victory was the Crowning Glory for the Thatcherite Programme. But, like all true Crowning Glories, it was not set up.

The Great Endorsement duly followed, with a thumping 144 majority in a general election the next year. The Programme, now in its Pomp, got into full gear.

There had been small privatizations in the first Thatcher government, but a Programme's Pomp is the time when its Action Plan gets fully realized. The sale of British Telecom, in 1984, then the biggest state sale of shares ever, raised nearly £4 billion. There were many sceptics, but the sale was a big success. It launched a new era of 'popular capitalism', and it also shook up the complacent Post Office – getting a phone installed in your home or business in the 1970s had been a nightmare. Other privatizations included British Gas (with its adverts telling 'Sid' about it), British Airways, a large part of BP and, later, the nation's ten water utilities. The model was copied around the world.

Entrepreneurship was encouraged. The Enterprise Allowance Scheme gave £40 a week to unemployed people starting a business – 325,000 people benefited from this. The Small Firms Loan Guarantee Scheme helped small firms borrow from banks. The top rate of tax was cut from 83% to 40% – though arguably the biggest beneficiaries of this were not entrepreneurs but in the City, where salaries boomed after the 1986 'Big Bang'. Perhaps the biggest boost to enterprise came from the change of tone. Entrepreneurs were suddenly feted. Sir Richard Branson, one of the most successful of them, said of Thatcher, "She really did set the groundwork for entrepreneurialism in Britain."

Time for the Big Battles with the trade unions. There were two such conflicts: the year-long miners' strike of 1984/5 and the even longer print-workers' strike of 1986/7. The former was the most dramatic, while the latter was arguably more emblematic of changing times, with Fleet Street printers resisting the introduction of new technology. Both involved violence at scary levels. Neither could have been won without a Great Endorsement.

Another Big Battle, in the international version of the First Story, was with the Soviet Empire. The fall of the Berlin Wall in 1989 was arguably the Programme's ultimate Big Win, six years into its Pomp. This was, of course, an allied effort, not just a British one. But Thatcher sympathized more and worked more closely with US President Ronald Reagan than did any other European leader. When deployed in 1983, more US cruise missiles were put in Britain than in any other European country. She then led the way in dealing with Mikhail Gorbachev, inviting him to Chequers in 1984, long before he met Reagan face-to-face.

One can argue that, once the old era of oil-based heavy industry had been replaced by the agile new one of IT, the oil-rich, heavy-industry-loving Soviet Union was doomed. But dying empires can be vicious. The end of the Cold War was a relatively gentle affair. That almost bloodless victory was an outstanding achievement, in which Mrs Thatcher played a key role. (Sadly, the usual narcissistic rage of collapsing empires seems not to have been soothed in 1989, but repressed. It is acting itself out now, instead.)

The Programme's economic liberalism was not matched in the social sphere. The apartheid regime in South Africa was tolerated, and even welcomed as a strategic ally. Homosexuality wasn't recriminalized, but a bizarre section in the 1988 Local Government Act insisted that Local Authorities should not 'intentionally promote' it. 'Promoting' was interpreted as any attempt to educate young people about the reality of different sexual orientations. (To be fair to the Programme, when the AIDS pandemic broke out, Britain led the way in public education, with the cabinet overriding the homophobic prejudices of many backbenchers and the Tory press.)

Culturally, the Thatcher years saw the rise of the Yuppie. Many young people no longer wanted to find their own way, as they had done in the late sixties and the seventies, but to do whatever was required in order to make money. Money, regarded as a bit grubby in the 1970s, suddenly conferred status. Yuppies could be of either gender; women reached out for power and took it, 'power dressing' to make the point.

Waves of brassy blockbuster movies flowed across the Atlantic. Popular music became smart and snappy, with synths and drum machines elbowing out guitars and wild, long-haired drummers (the first commercially available drum machine, the Linn LM-1, came out in 1980, the same year that Led Zeppelin's John Bonham died). Watch Duran Duran going sailing in 1982 on the video for *Rio*. Are those suits waterproof? Probably not, but they are very 'eighties'.

There was also a strong Counterblast. Songs like The Specials' *Ghost Town* protested the economic damage caused by the refusal to reflate. In the world of 'higher' culture, Mrs Thatcher had a small group of supporters, such as former Angry Young Man Kingsley Amis, novelist Anthony Powell and poet Philip Larkin, but the majority opinion was one of horror. The rising young novelists of the era, such as Amis' son Martin, Julian Barnes or Salman Rushdie, despised her. Critics of high culture said that just showed how stuck-up its exponents were. One certainly has to look hard to see any literary novel or serious film from the era that treats the adventure of entrepreneurship with the sensitivity that Peter Smith and Dilip Hiro's *A Private Enterprise* did back in 1974. *My Beautiful Laundrette*, from 1985, comes closest. The only established art where the Programme had real influence was architecture, where the functional 60s and 70s modernism associated with Wilsonian planning (and construction in the Soviet bloc) came under attack, and a new, flamboyant post-modern style blossomed.

At the 1989 Party Conference, delegates chanted "Ten More Years!" But Political Programmes don't last that long.

Thatcherism's First Big Failure was the Community Charge, better known as the poll tax. This was the culmination of a long-running battle between the Programme and its opponents in high-spending local councils. Councils were partially funded by 'rates' levied on homeowners and businesses. The Conservatives had long considered this unfair, but there was no agreement on how to replace them. One idea, suggested early on in the Programme's life, was a poll tax, levied equally on every adult. This was rejected as even more unfair: the very poor would be supposed to stump up exactly the same as the very rich. There had been no such taxes in England since the seventeenth century (an earlier one, in 1381, had led to armed revolution).

The battle between the government and far-left councils intensified over the decade, and finally the Conservatives decided to introduce a poll tax after all. This was done with some misgivings, but the PM was adamant. In 1987, she went as far as to declare that the new tax was the 'flagship of the Thatcher fleet'.

The tax was introduced in Scotland in 1989 (the Scottish Conservatives had been particularly strong advocates of the tax). The reaction to it was immediate and negative, with many people refusing to pay.

Time to drop the idea. But, of course, Mrs Thatcher was not a U-turner. Instead, the tax was rolled out in England and Wales the next year – and was a disaster. A large protest rally in Central London turned into a riot, but more seriously, huge swathes of the population objected. One opinion poll said that 75% of the population were against the tax. Labour began to roar ahead in the polls… But the fleet sailed on, heading straight for the rocks.

Clearly, Admiral Thatcher should have changed tack.

At this point, readers might object that my model says that Political Programmes shouldn't make U-turns, as Heath did. Am I now saying Thatcher should have made one?

There is a crucial difference between the two situations. For all the talk of 'flagships', the poll tax was not at the heart of the Programme's Big New Idea, which was about enterprise. The tax was not a Core Policy presented to, and massively endorsed by the electorate. It was a piece of Normal Politics, a policy added to a to-do list late in the career of that Programme. Yes, it was in the 1987 Tory manifesto, but right near the end – a very odd place for a 'flagship' policy. As a piece of Normal Politics, the poll tax could have been ditched without damaging the essential core of Thatcherism, just the ego of the Leader.

The Worldviews and Action Plans of full-on Political Programmes have a Darwinian robustness. They are forged in heated debate, then have to battle for wider acceptance: first within the party, then among the electorate, who will be sceptical to start with, but are finally won over. 'Normal' policy ideas, thought up to respond to newly emerging problems, do not have the same harsh evolutionary history. They may turn out to be genuinely good – but they may not.

An example of a piece of Normal Politics that worked well was Harold Macmillan's decolonization of Africa. This was never part of a Tory manifesto, and many old-school Tories loathed it – but, given the change of global mood over the 1950s, it was wise. Macmillan was flexible enough to accept this. (The nations that emerged have not had it easy, but it is sobering to compare them with Zimbabwe, which, as 'Rhodesia', opted out of the Macmillan approach, stuck with colonialist rule, and ended up with a bloody revolution, tyranny and hyper-inflation.)

The poll tax was, by contrast, a piece of Normal Politics that did not work well. Treated like a Core Policy and forced through against the popular will (and common sense), it effectively holed the Thatcher fleet.

The actual issue on which she was manoeuvred out of office was Europe. During the 1980s, Thatcher had been a key player in Europe, supporting a British Commissioner, Lord Cockfield, in designing the Single Market. But as the decade wore on, she became more and more concerned about the desire of the European Commission to centralize political power. When Commission President Jacques Delors claimed that within 10 years, 80% of the laws in Europe would be made at the European level, that was too much for her. Shortly after (in September 1988) she gave a speech in Bruges, where she laid into the idea of a 'European super-state'. This would become a Sacred Text for a later Programme.

The Party then had its Big Split, between pro- and anti-Europeans. This culminated in her being driven, reluctantly, from office in November 1990, after a damning parliamentary speech by former minister Sir Geoffrey Howe, and a leadership contest.

A classic Replacement Leader, John Major, was chosen. His TV persona was comically drab, but in real life he was sharp and witty. He was broadminded, actively disliking racial prejudice. His pleasant character probably won him a close election in 1992 (as Clement Attlee showed, British electors can warm to decent, quiet people). However, his 21-seat win in April 1992 was no Great Endorsement.

His success did not last long. In September of that year, the Programme that he had inherited took its Body-blow, when it crashed out of the European Exchange Rate Mechanism, a group of European currencies that tried to keep their values similar to one another. Major, then chancellor, had joined it in 1990, hoping it would keep inflation down. But 'Black Wednesday', September 16th, saw speculators shorting sterling, the government blowing billions of pounds trying to support it and failing. Interest rates shot up to 1970s levels, which terrified the life out of mortgaged homeowners.

A core part of Thatcherism's appeal had lain in the sense that the Conservatives 'got' the centrality of the economy and were good at managing it, unlike 'head in the clouds' Socialist dreamers (their Worldview, not mine). After Black Wednesday, that no longer rang true. Ironically, the economy did well in the later part of the Major years, but perception is a key aspect of politics.

Black Wednesday also exacerbated the Big Split. Tory Pro-Europeans and Eurosceptics hadn't exactly liked each other before September 16th, but the events of that day ramped up the antipathy. Eurosceptics now carried on a running battle with the administration as it tried to ratify the EU's Maastricht Treaty in parliament. After the ratification finally succeeded, in July 1993, a tape was left running after an interview: Major was heard referring to three Eurosceptic ministers as 'bastards'.

The Programme was now a Degenerating one. 'Europe' was one of its Slow Stranglers. Another was 'sleaze', a set of scandals about senior Tory figures' private lives and financial dealings. This was an own-goal. At the Split-riven 1993 Party Conference, Major made a speech about getting 'back to basics'. He was talking about old-fashioned decency and kindness in public life – an appeal that came naturally to him. But many in his party, including its Director of Communications, took it as a rallying cry to 'roll back the permissive society' and return to old-fashioned values: no sex before marriage, fidelity after it and a disapproval of homosexuality. Major, now desperate to maximize party unity, didn't disabuse these people of this misunderstanding: the rollers-back of permissiveness were often also Eurosceptics, and this was some way of appearing to share ground with them.

PR disasters soon followed. Two weeks later, it was revealed that a junior Tory minister, recently split from his wife, had three lovers, none of whom knew of the others' existence, and had had two other lovers while still married. This earned him some admiration for his energy, but none for his authenticity in spouting an anti-permissive message. Another MP who had talked of 'reducing the number of single parents' turned out to have an illegitimate child himself.

Another aspect of 'basics' was financial probity. A series of scandals – 'arms for Iraq', 'cash for questions' – quickly put paid to the administration's reputation for this.

Arguably, a third Slow Strangler was Northern Ireland, where progress towards peace seemed painfully slow. Major tried his best, as always, but there was too much historic distrust on the Republican side. Since 1912, the Conservatives had been technically called the 'Conservative and Unionist Party', and the party had been associated with Unionism a long time before that. Back in the reign of Queen Victoria, keeping the whole of Ireland in the UK had been a Core Policy of the Political Programme of Conservative Lord Salisbury, who won a Great Endorsement for it in 1895, from voters in Britain and Ulster, anyway. (It was Salisbury's Programme that the New Liberals had replaced in 1906.)

As happens when a Programme (or what's left of it) is Degenerating, a few Bright Ideas were mooted. The National Lottery was a big success. The Citizens' Charter was supposed to be a way of making public service providers more accountable: while it was not a bad idea in theory, many people complained that what public services needed was better funding, and it sank from view. The Cones Hotline got plenty of attention – of the wrong kind. This service, where motorists could call a number if they thought there were unnecessary restrictions during road works, was treated as a joke from the beginning. It may be an urban myth that it got loads of calls asking for a 99 with a Flake, but knowing the British delight in slightly silly, subversive humour, that wouldn't surprise me.

However, in the early 1990s there was no real alternative to the 'Thatcherism Lite' model on offer. So, just as the cumbersome geocentric model of the universe dominated astronomy for the entire Middle Ages, the Programme limped along, retaining power but not really knowing what to do with it.

But finally the Labour Party got its act together and came up with a Big New Idea.

Thatcherism

Leader: Margaret Thatcher

Foil: Willie Whitelaw

Core Policies: Privatization, low taxes, monetarist macroeconomics, face down trade unions, encourage entrepreneurship

Crucible Group: Centre for Policy Studies

Sacred Texts: Smith, Hayek, Friedman, the 'Ten Cannots'

Heroes: Anyone with economic aspirations, especially entrepreneurs

Villains: USSR, trade unions, 'scroungers', inflation, the state

Gaining Significant Influence: Thatcher becomes Party Leader, 1975

First Taste of Power: Election victory of 1979

Crowning Glory: Victory in the Falklands War

Great Endorsement: 144-seat victory in 1983

Cultural Endorsements (e.g.): *Rio* video, 1982. Quinlan Terry, *Richmond Riverside*

Counterblasts: *Ghost Town*, The Specials. *Money*, Martin Amis

Big Wins: Conquest of inflation, privatization, defeat of unions, Cold War

Big Battles: With NUM and print unions

First Big Failure: Poll tax

Body-blow: Black Wednesday, 16th September, 1992

Slow Stranglers: Europe, 'back to basics'/sleaze, Northern Ireland

Dethronement/Waterloo: Labour landslide of 1997

New Labour, 1997 - 2010

I'm not sure there was a Sacred Text for this Programme. Maybe parts of Crosland's *Future of Socialism* qualify, where he talked of the need for a brighter Britain. Or Jenkins' *Labour Case*. Sociologist Anthony Giddens, who wrote a number of books at the start of the 1990s about a 'Third Way' between socialism and capitalism, influenced many Programme supporters – but the Programme Leader, Tony Blair, makes no reference to him in his autobiography.

More influential on Blair was European civilization's original Sacred Text, the Bible. One has to go back to Stanley Baldwin to find a Programme Leader for whom Christianity mattered as much. Blair's faith was very different to that of the pipe-smoking Tory gentleman. Strongly influenced by philosopher John Macmurray and Peter Thomson, a rebellious Australian mature student he met at Oxford, it was egalitarian and anti-establishment.

Or maybe the Sacred Texts weren't written texts at all but 60s and 70s rock, with its insistence on emotional intensity and personal authenticity. Blair tried his hand as a music promoter as a young man, then sang in a student band. There is a great divide between people who came of age in the fifties/early-1960s and those who did so in the late-1960s/seventies. Blair was the first UK Programme Leader to be on the modern side of that divide.

There was no Crucible Group, either. The nearest thing was a Crucible duet. As a newly-elected MP in 1983, Blair shared an office with another new arrival, Gordon Brown, and they spent many hours discussing all aspects of policy. Both were seen as 'men with a future' in the party. Initially, Brown, who was slightly older and had deeper roots in the Labour movement, was looked on as the potential leader. But Blair edged past him. After the untimely death of party leader John Smith in 1994, Blair ran for leadership. He reputedly did a deal with Brown over dinner at a restaurant in New Labour's spiritual home, Islington, that if he (Brown) did not stand against him, he (Blair) would give Brown considerable power and would hand over the PM's job to him after two terms in office.

Blair then won the leadership race, via a convoluted process, at the end of that year. The Programme had acquired Significant Influence.

During this time, he gathered an Action group around him: himself, Brown, Alistair Campbell, Peter Mandelson, PR expert Anji Hunter and former diplomat Jonathan Powell.

Blair consolidated his power in the party. Clause IV, its 77-year-old commitment to massive nationalization, was abolished in 1995. In pursuit of electoral victory, he even wooed right-wing media mogul Rupert Murdoch.

In 1997, New Labour leapfrogged any gentle First Taste of Power and jumped straight to a Great Endorsement – the greatest in the post-war era – seizing total, confident control in a landslide electoral win. The 179-seat majority was the biggest for a political party since Baldwin's in 1924, bigger than anything achieved by Attlee or Thatcher.

Maybe it is the case that the longer the previous Programme limps along after its Body-blow, the more likely it is that a new one will leap straight to a Great Endorsement.

Blair's Programme has been accused of being light on policy, but this is unfair. Maybe it listened to focus groups too much, but that was mainly about tweaking Normal Politics. It had a clear Worldview and Action Plan and stuck to it for a long time.

The Worldview had much more respect for market mechanisms than previous Labour Programmes, which had seen them as wild, amoral things which needed planning. Thatcherism, by contrast, had made of a fetish of the markets: the hidden hand could do no wrong. New Labour sought a genuine middle way, admiring markets' (and especially entrepreneurs') capacity to generate wealth but also understanding that markets are not perfectly efficient or always morally good. Money would be spent on 'public goods' such as health and education. A new marriage of private and public sector was planned.

However, the heart of their Worldview was cultural and social. Unlike Thatcherism, which had introduced the anti-gay Section 28 legislation and, while limping along, come up with 'back to basics', New Labour championed diversity, difference and inclusiveness. There were twice as many women in the new parliament than in the previous one – 101 out of the 120 being on the Labour benches. Homophobia and racism were taboo (though parliament still had few black, Asian or minority-ethnic MPs). The Programme set a radically fresh tone: tolerant, young, metropolitan, intelligent, able, international, open, emotionally literate.

The Programme rode the wave of a new burst of cultural creativity. Louis de Bernières' big-spirited novel *Captain Corelli's Mandolin* and Richard Curtis' unashamedly romantic movie *Four Weddings and a Funeral* (with its opening salvo of f-words that horrified the Thatcher generation) both date from 1994, the year of Blair's conquest of the Labour Party. De Bernières' three previous novels had been in the niche 'magical realism' genre, but *Captain Corelli* spoke to a wider readership. Unlike the self-consciously literary Counterblast prizewinners of the 1980s, such as Salman Rushdie, Martin Amis and Julian Barnes, *Corelli* was both literary and delightfully approachable – a symbol of a new, mass 'small l' liberalism. It was a favourite with Book Clubs, a key cultural phenomenon of the Blair era, which kicked off in America with Oprah Winfrey's club in 1996, but soon flourished over here.

Similarly, the great 'Britpop' acts, Blur, Oasis and Pulp, battled it out in the last days of the Major administration but were heralds of the world of New Labour. The same can be said for the club, Ministry of Sound, and the feisty Spice Girls, who had stormed the charts in 1996.

The year of the Programme's Great Endorsement, 1997, saw the first volume of the Harry Potter series with its strong messages of anti-racism and individual empowerment cloaked in the kind of witty fantasy that hard-headed Thatcherites despised. Harry Potter was for the new Programme what The Beatles had been for Harold Wilson in 1964: a global advertisement, infinitely more powerful than any political speeches or GDP figures, that new-look Britain was onto something. The media talked of 'Cool Britannia'.

There was very little Counterblast.

Arguably, the new Programme had a Crowning Glory a couple of nights after its landslide, when the UK's Katrina and the Waves stormed to an equally large victory in the Eurovision Song Contest. Europe was watching the new government and approved (*Love, Shine a*

Light was also a fine song, performed with gusto by a tremendous singer – sadly, not always the case with UK Eurovision entries).

However, on home ground, the Programme's uninvited triumph came with the death of Princess Diana. Four months after Blair's victory, the nation awoke to the news – and responded in a way that the British public had never done before. Early that morning, a few people came to lay flowers outside Kensington Palace. That soon turned into to a flood. Blair was asked to respond to the death, and gave a simple but heartfelt speech. (One can never tell with professional politicians, but when he said he was 'utterly devasted', the look on his face seemed to match the words. Watch the video.)

The flowers in front of Kensington and then Buckingham Palaces became a lake and then a sea. It was clear that the nation was expressing grief in a totally new way. There was a sense that the people of the UK had been to a therapy session, asked to look at their own buried unhappinesses, and had suddenly burst into floods of tears.

Blair intuitively understood and respected this: by contrast, the Conservative Party looked wooden and embarrassed. One felt that it wanted to slap Britain round the face and tell the nation to bloody well snap out of it. The party also had a young leader at the time, William Hague, but he was bemused by the public reaction. One of his older colleagues, a former member of John Major's cabinet, told journalist Matthew D'Ancona: "I walked through the crowds in St James's, and realised this was no longer a country I truly understand."

It seems odd to talk of this as a Glory, but it was an unscripted mass demonstration of emotion exactly in tune with the tone of the newly endorsed Political Programme, which is what a Crowning Glory is.

The new government soon secured some Big Wins.

In 1998, a national minimum wage was introduced. As at the start of Thatcherism, a number of economists said this policy wouldn't work but this was ignored. The policy has been retained ever since.

The same year saw the Good Friday Agreement in Northern Ireland. New governmental institutions were set up in the province: the Northern Ireland Assembly and Executive, with the latter based on 'power-sharing' between Unionists and Irish Nationalists (as opposed to a system where a majority ruled the roost). Bodies were created to facilitate dialogue between Eire and the Six Counties and between Eire and Britain. Most important of all, the major paramilitary organizations agreed to renounce violence. After three decades of horrific killings, this was a massive achievement.

Other Big Wins include the setting up of the Sure Start programme for nurseries, the creation of a separate government department for International Development and a genuine redistribution of wealth via changes to the tax and benefits system. According to Matt Beech and Simon Lee, two academics at Hull University, around 2 million people were lifted out of poverty by New Labour.

History, of course, was waiting, Voldemort-like, to trip up the new Programme. New Labour had a long, vigorous Pomp, but its First Big Failure duly arrived in 2003, when the Leader went to war in Iraq. He did so with hardly any support with our European allies, and against the wishes of a million people who marched through London on February 15th to protest.

There was a quick, impressive military victory – followed by helpless, ever-deepening entanglement in Iraqi politics. There had been inadequate planning as to what would happen after we won, and our intended liberation of that complex, divided country soon turned into occupation. This became a recruiting-call for terrorists, especially after the interrogation procedures at Abu Ghraib prison became public knowledge. This had a horrific pay-off with the 2005 London attacks.

After the war, no Weapons of Mass Destruction (WMD) were found in Iraq. Suspicion began to grow that a dossier produced by the government in September 2002, purportedly full of objective information about the country's possession of WMD, had been 'sexed up' to promote the war. A whistleblower, Dr David Kelly, was found dead in July 2003 – most likely a case of suicide, but suicide brought on by political pressure placed on him.

Blair's personal credibility was seriously damaged. His reputation for competence suffered from the disastrous occupation. His reputation for honesty – a major part of his appeal in 1997, contrasting with 'Tory sleaze' – suffered from the suspicions about the dossier, even though he was later officially cleared of any wrongdoing. New Labour had always relied heavily on 'spin', on the framing and selection of facts to prove a case. Many people thought the dossier had crossed the boundary between spin and outright lying.

However, the Programme carried on. In its third election, in 2005, its majority was cut by more than half, but it was still a tidy 66 seats.

Iraq has to be seen as a 'First Big Failure', not a Body-blow. That was the financial crash of 2007/8. Old Labour had seen the City as a posh casino, the home of privileged speculators, with more loyalty to those Zurich gnomes than to the nation. To New Labour, it was an essential part of the modern economy, providing 'financial services'. It made huge amounts of money that was spent in booming London and that could be taxed to support worthwhile projects like the NHS, Sure Start or Tax Credits. The markets in which the City operated were seen not as casino tables but essentially safe mechanisms for efficiently allocating capital. They were seen as containing enormous amounts of wisdom, more than any individual or even body of individuals could access. Maybe in the old days there had been spectacular crashes, but New Labour knew better. The dotcom boom and bust around the turn of the millennium had shown this: it had been dramatic but the economy had quickly recovered. New Labour essentially carried forward the Thatcherite approach to the City, which was to keep it deregulated.

Blair handed over power to his former lieutenant Gordon Brown on 27 June 2007. Like Ted Heath, the newcomer was unlucky with his timing. Two months later, Northern Rock, a once aptly-named old-style building society that had embraced the new world of financial deregulation and turned itself into a rather racy bank offering 125% mortgages, went bust. In March 2008, Bear Stearns, the most risk-loving of Wall Street's big investment banks, followed suit. Then in September of that year, Lehmann Brothers, an institution with a theoretically much more solid reputation, filed for bankruptcy. Royal Bank of Scotland, which had embarked on a decade-long acquisition spree based on debt, looked set to follow it. Suddenly the entire financial system looked about to come crashing down in a rerun, not of the dotcom flurry but of the catastrophe of the 1930s.

Brown handled the crisis superbly. Arguably he did more to save the global financial system than anyone else. Huge amounts of money were thrown, decisively and quickly, at debt-ridden banks to prevent runs on them. The system pulled through. (Some critics say that the system should have been reformed at the same time. No doubt, but right then, this was all about simple survival.)

So wasn't this a triumph for New Labour? The crisis was global, not just national, and Brown had been at the heart of the rescue operation. However, the 2008 crash destroyed core beliefs in the Programme's Worldview, that markets could always be relied upon and that the City was a risk-free tax cow. It also left the nation with a level of debt not seen since the 1960s, when we were still paying off the cost of World War Two. In the Worldview of the Blairite Political Programme, there was only one way to reduce this debt: cut expenditure and then plod painfully back to a more sustainable debt level. Cue 'austerity', which placed much of the burden of the debt recovery on the poor and soon became the Slow Strangler for the Programme.

A second Strangler was the Programme's tone. A sense developed that its metropolitan leaders looked down on older, provincial types, especially males, secretly considering them racist, sexist, homophobic, vulgarly nationalistic and generally obsolete. This perceived dismissiveness was summed up in an incident during the 2010 election campaign, when Gillian Duffy, a 65-year-old retired council worker who had lived in Rochdale (and voted Labour) all her life, questioned Gordon Brown on a number of issues, including immigration from Eastern Europe. After talking to her, a microphone picked up Brown complaining that she should not have been let near him, adding, "She was just a bigoted woman."

Such condescension had been foreseen in Michael Young's *The Rise of the Meritocracy* back in 1958. 'Meritocracy' (a word he invented) is often thought of as desirable, better than old fashioned class advantage, but the book was actually a warning. Young's meritocrats were ruthless. The old class overlords, like most Fifties Conservatives, had possessed a sense of *noblesse oblige*. Meritocrats, Young reckoned, would have no such sense. They reckoned they had earned their status and felt free to despise the less successful.

The same warning has recently been reissued by American philosopher Michael J Sandel in *The Tyranny of Merit*.

Labour lost the 2010 election, and a hung parliament resulted. This marked the end of the Programme – but in some ways it lived on, only finally meeting its Waterloo in 2019, when radically new voices forced their way to the fore.

New Labour

Leader: Tony Blair
Foil: Gordon Brown
Sacred Texts: (?) The work of Anthony Giddens
Core Policies: Social liberalism, inclusivity, 'Market Socialism'
Carried Forward: Respect for enterprise, a deregulated City
Crucible Group: Blair and Brown
Action Group: Them plus Mandelson, Campbell, Hunter, Powell
Heroes: The 'new man', post-feminist woman
Gaining Significant Influence: Blair becomes party Leader
First Taste of Power: Election victory of 1997
Great Endorsement: The same (!)
Crowning Glory: Public mourning for Diana, Princess of Wales
Cultural Endorsement: *Captain Corelli's Mandolin*, *Four Weddings and a Funeral*, Harry Potter books and movies, 'Cool Britannia'
Big Wins: Minimum wage, Good Friday Agreement, Increased NHS spending, Tax credits
First Big Failure: Iraq War (2003) and aftermath
Body-blow: 2008 crash
Slow Stranglers: Austerity, disconnect with provincial Labour voters
Dethronement: 2010 election
Waterloo: 2019 election

The Coalition Years, 2010 - 2015

A few dramatic days followed the 2010 result, at the end of which a Coalition was agreed between the Conservatives (who had received most votes and most seats) and the Liberal Democrats.

Together, the two parties had a majority of 72. A Great Endorsement? I find it hard to argue that the administration was a proper Political Programme. The electorate hadn't fully endorsed either of the parties – the 'endorsement' came simply from adding together two groups of people who had voted for different leaders and policies.

The Coalition carried forward much of the spirit of New Labour (participants in that administration may disagree). Both the Conservatives' David Cameron and his Lib Dem colleague Nick Clegg were chips off the Blair block: young, London-based, cultured, intelligent, internationally-minded and socially liberal. Cameron saw himself as a modernizer of his Party, just as Blair had modernized his. Under his watch, the number of female Conservative MPs doubled (just as the number of female Labour MPs had doubled under Blair). He got popular culture: unlike Blair he never fronted a band, but unlike most Thatcher-era Tory figures, he liked popular music, citing Mancunian miserabilists The Smiths as his favourite band was when he was a teenager.

The Conservatives' ideas were based around Cameron's notion of the 'Big Society'. This marked a major shift from Thatcherism, whose leader had notably said there was 'no such thing' as society. There was a belief that 'the days of big government' were over. Decision-making would be pushed away from Westminster and closer to citizens ('big citizens', according to a document issued by the Coalition shortly after its formation). Rather than boss citizens around, the government would 'nudge' them into more helpful behaviours, such as healthy eating.

The Liberal Democrats had a new Sacred Text, *The Orange Book (Reclaiming Liberalism)*. This recast liberalism from a centre-left movement (the way it had been since the last time it had truly led a full-on Political Programme, from 1906 to 1916) to one much more favourable to the free market. At the same time, they retained their commitment to individual liberty. Gladstone would have approved. They now had a First Taste of Power – their first, since 1922. Next step, a Great Endorsement?

Policies included the beefing up of the apprenticeship system, the introduction of a 'pupil premium' to help schools in poorer areas, the legalization of same-sex marriage and a commitment to spend 0.7% of GNP on overseas aid. All of these were (in my view, anyway) admirable.

Less admirable, and less liberal, was the 'Hostile Environment' policy of the Home Office, designed to put off illegal immigrants, but which adversely affected many legal ones.

Worst of all, the Programme generated no fresh policies for the biggest problem faced by the country at the time, which was the debt burden left over from the financial crisis. This was, to use a metaphor popular at the time, 'the elephant in the room'. Instead, the administration just ploughed on with austerity, cutting spending on the provision of public goods, which duly became a Slow Strangler for it. As a result, 'The Big Society' started to feel more and more like a Slogan.

There was very little spontaneous Cultural Endorsement for the new administration. The determination of Cameron and Clegg to work together was generally liked, but there was no sense of a blast of radical fresh air. Coalition had a pleasant vibe, but wasn't invigorating, in the way that full-on, new Political Programmes are.

Culturally, the most significant mood was probably of Counterblast. Ken Loach's movie, *I, Daniel Blake*, which described the battles of a well-meaning working-class man against the bureaucracy of the benefit system, was written during the Coalition era, though it actually appeared on the screen in 2016.

And, of course, the business of coalition is not easy. The Liberals were quickly forced to do a U-turn on one of their Core election policies. Having campaigned to get rid of university tuition fees, they conceded to their partners and allowed the administration to put them up substantially. This would prove fatal to them at the next election. (The moral of that story is not 'never enter coalition', but 'if you do enter coalition, be prepared to walk away if a policy is insisted on that runs counter to one of your Core ones'.)

Arguably, the administration had a Crowning Glory, the 2012 London Olympics. However, these were a New Labour idea. The Games are, perhaps, better seen as a celebration of a mindset that straddled both New Labour and the Coalition. Danny Boyle and Frank Cottrell Boyce's opening ceremony was a magnificent love letter to the (then) modern nation. It was quirky, diverse, passionate, moving and infused with that great British virtue, humour. The multi-ethnic Team GB performed brilliantly, coming third in the table with 29 gold medals. (A few Olympics earlier, at Atlanta in 1996, we had won one gold, thanks to rowers Steve Redgrave and Matthew Pinsent, putting us 36th in the medals table.) As the fireworks lit up the East London sky at the closing ceremony – an event watched by a TV audience of 26 million, a figure second only to Princess Diana's funeral – one could be forgiven for thinking that austerity was just a passing phase. Administrations would come and go, but Britain had found its tone for the new century: youthful, creative, curious, outward-looking, broad-minded and ambitious, intellectually and emotionally.

Nothing is forever in politics. The Olympics were more a swansong than a coronation. Other voices were demanding to be heard.

The Coalition Years

Leaders: David Cameron (Conservative), Nick Clegg (Lib Dem)
Carried forward: Youthful attitude, sophistication, social liberalism
Core Policies: Devolve power from state to citizen
Sacred Text: (for Lib Dems) *The Orange Book*
First Taste of Power: 2010 election victory
Crowning Glory: (?) 2012 Olympics
Counterblast: Ken Loach, *I, Daniel Blake*
Slow Strangler: Austerity
Body-blow: (for Lib Dems) introduction of student fees
Dethronement: 2015 election
Waterloo: 2019 election

Populist 'Brexit' Nationalism, 2016 - present

All democratic Political Programmes are popul*ar*. They resonate with and act upon a strong set of emotions felt and ideas held by a huge swathe of the population. That is how they get their Great Endorsement, which in turn is what gives them the legitimacy to do the tough things they have to do.

Popul*ism* takes a particular line. It is actively anti-elite, regarding the people at the top at best as complacent and out of touch and at worst as 'rent-seeking', feathering their own nests while working hard to protect their privilege. In contrast to such perceived elite ineptness and/or hypocrisy, populism celebrates the man and woman in the street, out there in the thick of it, doing 'the real work' day in, day out. These Heroes (of either gender) are seen as having innate moral virtues: honesty, a sense of fairness, a strong work ethic and loyalty to community and nation.

The last of these is particularly important. Populism and nationalism almost always go hand in hand, and certainly did in the storytelling of this Programme.

The core issue around which British (or at least English and Ulster Protestant) nationalism coalesced was our membership of the European Union. For years, surveys have shown the UK public to be the least European-minded of all EU members. (The surveys, carried out by Eurobarometer, failed to distinguish between the nations of the UK. I'm sure they would have found more support for the EU in Scotland.) Yet, even in England, our feelings were more of apathy than active antipathy. In the early Blair years, the UK moved in close step with political Europe, though Gordon Brown drew the line at joining the Euro. Most people seemed quite happy. Sort-of in, sort-of out: a nice, very British compromise.

Some people were not happy, of course. They hadn't been for a long time, as John Major had found out when trying to get the Maastricht Treaty ratified.

Arguably the first full-on Eurosceptic Crucible Group was the Bruges Group, named after Thatcher's 1988 speech, which was a Sacred Text for this Programme. Founded by an Oxford student, Patrick Robertson, the group soon attracted big names, such as former president of the IEA, Ralph Harris. In 1990, Mrs Thatcher became its honorary president. It has continued to publish papers ever since. Within the Conservative Party, opposition to the EU (as it was called after 1992) coalesced into the European Research Group, founded in 1993 by MP Michael Spicer.

An early Eurosceptic Action Group was founded by academic Alan Sked (who was also a member of the Bruges Group) in 1991. His Anti-Federalist League put up candidates in the 1992 election – and hardly got any votes. The party was renamed UKIP in 1993. For a while, it was eclipsed by a newer anti-EU party, the Referendum Party, bankrolled by magnate Sir James Goldsmith. This, too, failed at the polls (in 1997). It then disappeared, leaving UKIP to pick up the flickering Eurosceptic torch again.

For a long while after that, Brexiter Crucible Groups churned out papers which were eagerly read by other Eurosceptics, while UKIP stood in elections and just managed to outperform the full-on joke candidates (it did increase its share of the vote, from 1.5% in 2001 to 2.2% in 2005). But in 2006, the charismatic Nigel Farage became party leader. Things began to change.

The 2008 crash, caused by a London-based elite of bankers with close ties to government, and the financial scandals of the following year, where swathes of MPs were discovered to have been highly creative with their expenses claims, helped the populist mood. However, a glance at Mark Pack's exhaustive 'PollBase' list of opinion polls shows that the effect of these was minor, and that the real explosion of support for UKIP came not in 2008/9 but in 2012/3. From regular ratings of around 5% before March 2012, it tripled to 15% or more twelve months later. In October 2014, the party won its first by-election, ex-Tory Douglas Carswell winning a stunning 59.7% of the votes. This was the second biggest election swing in UK political history. Something was stirring.

What exactly? Farage had been working hard on widening the party's appeal, from specific anti-Europeanism to wider populist themes of anti-elitism and anti-immigration. The latter, sadly, seems to have been a powerful force: the early 2010s saw rising concern at immigration into the EU from Africa and the Middle East.

However, none of those factors totally explains the rise. The Zeitgeist moves in a mysterious way. Set up by long-term pressures, enthusiasm for an Aspirant Programme can seethe and bubble for a long while, then suddenly make a great leap forward for no obvious reason. Memo to anyone seeking to create a Political Programme: if your ideas have what it takes, this will happen. Keep on spreading your message with passion and confidence. Things will be stirring, even if there is limited evidence for that. Suddenly, for reasons you can't quite understand, people will start turning round and saying "Yes! Of course!"

This sudden rise in UKIP support panicked the Conservative leadership. In January 2013, the new Aspirant 'Brexit' Programme gained Significant Influence when David Cameron gave a speech promising a referendum on EU membership. He could not, of course, deliver one, as he was in coalition with the Euro-friendly Liberal Democrats (who by then must have been thinking that they should have teamed up with Labour back in 2010). But the promise was made, so if the Tories won the next election, due in 2015…

They did, with a small (12 seats) but clear majority. UKIP got 13% of the votes. The referendum was set for 23 June 2016.

There were various organizations on the Brexit side. The official one was Vote Leave, whose campaigning was led by Dominic Cummings. It used the latest data-capture and -analysis technology to target voters online, with extraordinary precision, and succeeded in galvanizing new votes – not the young, but older people who had given up hope in the system ever delivering anything for them. Clutches of newly-motivated voters are often a key part of a Democratic Revolution.

The nation voted (narrowly) to leave. This was the First Taste of Power for the new Programme. There had been no change in the parliamentary arithmetic, but from then on, the Brexiters ('Brexiteers' in the Programme's Stories, an extra *e* added to make their Heroes sound like buccaneers) were the most powerful force in the land.

However, the Programme still had to turn its First Taste of Power into full-on control. It had many powerful enemies and many detractors (who, as always at such times, underrated it). Cameron resigned after the defeat, but was not replaced with a Brexiter Populist but with Theresa May, a former 'Remain' supporter. Pro-EU activists took to the streets, with huge marches in London. The Programme's success was not guaranteed.

The Programme rose to the challenge. That's what true Political Programmes do. Mrs May possibly hoped to counteract it and aim for a deal with Europe, but she found herself pressurized by her party into taking an ever-tougher approach, drawing 'red lines' in all sorts of places that had been given little airtime during the actual campaign. During the Referendum, various models of life outside the EU had been mooted. Norway was part of the EU single market. Turkey was part of the customs union. Switzerland was part of the Schengen Zone (free movement across borders). The Programme, now in full cry, would have none of this. Its aim was a 'hard' Brexit, cutting the UK off from Europe as much as possible.

Some commentators remain puzzled by why Mrs May fell in line with this: she seems to have ditched all her previous beliefs. But such is the power of a Political Programme cresting the Zeitgeist. Her party was flocking round the new banner and she had little choice to do otherwise. Her time in office is best seen as a series of attempted compromise solutions, aimed at halting the rising 'hard Brexit' tide, which simply flowed past them. She was Queen Canute.

Her attempts ended after disastrous (for her) European Election results in May 2019, where the Conservatives were virtually annihilated and 29 of the 73 seats went to the Brexit Party, Farage's reinvention of UKIP. She resigned, tearfully, and the Conservatives chose Boris Johnson to take over – as they had to do: he had become the face and the voice (and the hairstyle) of Populist Nationalism. This was a Palace

Revolution, the first such revolution in this story not to have happened during a war. Like all Palace Revolutions, it was followed through with great ruthlessness. Instead of voters chucking out old-Programme MPs, the party did it for them. Some Tory Remainers left the party and attempted to form centrist parties, which soon evaporated. Others quit politics altogether, disillusioned or fearing deselection by eager, new-Programme-supporting constituency activists. (Losing Palace Revolutions is a nasty business. In Imperial China, mandarins who fell out of favour were often executed along with their families. The great historian Sima Qian, who fell foul of the Tang Dynasty Empress Wu, was castrated. There are worse fates than being a Tory Remainer.)

This was another step forward for the Programme, but what it really needed was a Great Endorsement.

In December 2019, it got it. Labour and the Lib Dems have been criticized for letting the 'Christmas' election happen. It certainly made little sense if one looked at the polls – and even less sense once the Brexit Party did its deal with the Conservatives, that it would not stand in Tory-held seats. But the country had to be asked if it really did want Brexit, not through another referendum but through the proper method of establishing public desire in a representative democracy, a general election. It went to the polls and delivered its answer, Johnson winning an unexpected 80 seat majority.

The Great Endorsement of the new Programme was Waterloo for the residual liberalism of both New Labour and the Coalition. It supporters tumbled into classic, ill-natured Dissolution-phase factionalism. JK Rowling, creator of the emblematic Harry Potter series, found herself under vicious attack from fellow progressives over her views on transgender rights.

What did the victorious new Programme look like?

In its First Story, the character in need of rescue was 'Workington Man', a stereotype created by the right-of-centre think-tank, Onward, and courted by the Conservatives in the 2019 election. He was an older, white, skilled working-class town-dweller, conservative socially and quietly but solidly patriotic. He was not ambitious culturally or career-wise, unlike the eager Wilsonian technocrat, the aspirational Thatcherite entrepreneur or the intellectually curious metropolitan Blairite. He was angry at the costs of austerity and what he believed to be the effects of immigration, especially from the EU: overstretched services and depressed wages. He wanted out of the Union, partially from nationalism and partly from a sense of fairness: 'Remain' had lost the referendum, and should admit defeat. (No 'Workington Woman' was posited at his side, though election pundits do talk about 'Worcester Woman', from the same class but younger and struggling financially to bring up two kids. Workington Man's daughter? But it was men who were targeted this time.)

The Villains? Populists love Villains, and this Programme had a healthy selection. The liberal metropolitan elite. The BBC. 'Experts' of all kinds, but particularly judges and, more recently, if you read the *Daily Mail,* GPs. 'Woke' activists. Immigrants (not demonized as openly as the above, but once in power, the Programme was eager to keep as many out as possible). The arch-Villain, based in its towering, glass-fronted, foreign headquarters: the European Commission.

Its Second Story? Initially this was clear. Brexit would clear the way for a new-look Britain, an aggressive competitor in global markets with a low-tax, low-regulation economy and a minimal state. This model was sometimes called 'Singapore on Thames', though the East Asian statelet is so radically different to the UK, culturally, historically and geographically, that this never made much sense.

This Story had its Sacred Text. *Britannia Unchained* is a collection of essays published in 2012 by five then up-and-coming MPs, four of whom are now in the cabinet and two of whom, Priti Patel and Liz Truss, hold Great Offices of State (another, Dominic Raab, is Deputy PM). In it, they celebrate a set of virtues. One is sound finance: the nation's debts must be paid off quickly and the books balanced from then on. Another is the enterprise economy (low taxation, minimal regulation). Another – I feel it's their favourite – is the work ethic: success comes from hard graft. The British worker, the book argues, has not been very good at this of late.

A different Second Story has emerged since then, more eager to spend money and less eager to criticize UK workers. More on this below.

The Programme has had two Leaders. Farage got the Big New Idea into the public consciousness, but was too much of a political outsider to finish the job. Johnson was needed to carry it on to its Great Endorsement.

Both men provide excellent examples of how Leaders of rising or victorious Political Programmes can say the previously unsayable. During the referendum campaign, Farage proudly posed in front of a poster showing a column of non-white refugees and the slogan 'Breaking Point'. Liberals gasped in horror; Farage just shrugged. Johnson has a history of throwaway comments about 'piccaninnies' or Muslim women in burqas looking like letter boxes. Such things would hobble the careers of most public figures – imagine a newsreader or the England football manager saying these things – but not these two.

They are the masters now – for the moment.

The Cultural Endorsement of the new Programme has come from the press, with the *Daily Express, Daily Mail* and *Daily Telegraph* leading the charge. Outside Fleet Street, however, there has been little such Endorsement. High culture is by definition an elite business; populists don't like elites and the dislike is reciprocated. Popular culture is largely driven by young people, who didn't vote for Brexit anyway (though a few old wild men of rock came out in favour of Brexit: Ringo Starr, The Who's Roger Daltrey, The Fall's contrarian Mark E Smith).

The Programme has decided to make a virtue of this and stoke up a Culture War, arguing that the reason why there has been such a narrow Cultural Endorsement is because one set of Villains, the liberal metropolitan elite, control both high and popular culture. The Programme presents itself as fighting back against this hegemony. Its sensible, hard-working, patriotic Heroes are contrasted with an idle 'chattering class' lacking in loyalty to anything other than themselves and to intellectual fad. The appointment of Nadine Dorries, the proudly lowbrow author of bestselling family sagas, as Secretary of State for Digital, Culture, Media and Sport, is the Programme's most recent move in this conflict.

Culture War is essentially an import from America, where it had been rumbling since the late 1960s but took off in 1992 thanks to the oratory of Republican Pat Buchanan. An early British expression of it was John Carey's *The Intellectuals and the Masses*, from the same year. However Carey is not Buchanan: the war has never been as impassioned – or, frankly, as bizarre – this side of the Atlantic. Will it work as a party political tool here? It has gone down a storm with the faithful, but research by Rebecca Benson and Bobby Duffy of the Kings College

London Policy Institute shows that 'Progressives' and 'Traditionalists', the two participants in the conflict, each make up about one quarter of the adult UK population, while the rest of us take a more nuanced position. Of these, most are 'Moderates', while the others, 'Disengaged', are not that fussed either way. The more strident the Programme's culture warriors get, the more the Moderates and the Disengaged are likely to be alienated.

The Programme's culture warriors are right to say that there are plenty of Counterblasts to the Programme. My favourite example was Banksy's mural, on the side of a house in Dover, of a workman chipping away to remove one star from an EU flag. I say 'was' because it has since been whitewashed over: both sides in the Culture War can cancel. More internationally, the mindset of nationalism is being challenged by organizations like Global Citizen. Online, young people have a culture where they make friends and play computer games with peers from all round the world. While they enjoy what I call 'gentle nationalism', they are well aware of other identities and enjoy diversity.

The Programme had its first Big Win on 31st January, 2020, when Britain formally left the EU, though aspects of the divorce remained to be sorted out.

A Crowning Glory to go with it? If there was one, it came late, for a reason which will become apparent below. England's successful run, all the way to the final, in the delayed UEFA Euro 2020 football championships saw Number Ten draped in St George's flags.

However, this wasn't 30th July 1966. England lost the game – by the narrowest of margins, a penalty shoot-out after extra time. But even if our penalties had gone in, the success of the diverse young team and its gentle, thoughtful manager Gareth Southgate belonged to a different world than that of the Programme. When the players took the knee before each game to protest against racism, they attracted negative comment from some Tories, boos from racists in the crowd, and repeated and ever more convoluted refusals from Johnson to explicitly condemn that booing. Yes, our run to the final and our sympathy for the young men put in the firing line in the penalty shoot-out did unite the country – but not quite in a way the Programme wanted.

The delay in this near-Crowing Glory was, of course, due to the pandemic. On the very day of that first Big Win, 31st January 2020, the first cases of the Covid-19 virus were announced in the UK. At first, this was a disaster for the new administration (not to mention tens of thousands of citizens). The government reacted slowly, despite getting plenty of warning from events in Italy. Johnson failed to attend vital COBRA meetings and then flouted medical advice by pointedly shaking hands with people to show what he thought of 'experts'. It nearly got him killed. Lockdown was slow, and infected individuals were shunted from hospitals into care homes, where the virus duly spread among already infirm people. Supplies of PPE were inadequate, and a trumpeted 'world-beating' test and trace system (typical of a newly endorsed Programme to be this boastful) turned out to be expensive and not very effective. Britain soon had one of the highest *per capita* case levels in the world. Yet there was only limited public fury about this – a classic Great Escape.

The pandemic then gave the Programme a Big Win. Once it was announced that a vaccine was being trialled, a Vaccine Taskforce was set up under businesswoman Kate Bingham. This proved highly effective. Economically, the government quickly abandoned Selsdon/Thatcherite notions of letting the weak go to the wall and created a massive support system for businesses forced to close due to lockdown. The success of the UK vaccine rollout was particularly pleasing for the Programme, as its arch-villain in Brussels was inept in trying to do the same thing, entering late into the vaccine market then stamping its little foot when it didn't get exactly what it wanted.

Populist 'Brexit' Nationalism only entered its Pomp in December 2019, so in theory it should still expect a few more Great Escapes. However, it already seems in trouble. Harold Wilson ran out of road quickly after his 1966 Great Endorsement, and the same may be happening now.

The Programme's 'honeymoon period' of huge poll leads lasted till mid-2020, after which the lead stabilized around 5%, with the odd up- and down-tick. This lead survived shortages in shops and petrol queues. But since the middle of October 2021, it has collapsed, and polls are now showing a 5% deficit. In December 2021 the Conservatives lost a by-election in a previously ultra-safe seat – the swing to the victorious Lib Dems was the seventh highest in UK electoral history, the sort of thing that normally only happens when a Programme is Degenerating.

The fall in the polls began with the Owen Paterson affair, when a former minister was found guilty of having breached lobbying rules, and, rather than following the usual course of suspending him, the administration tried to force through changes in those rules, in order to exonerate him. 'One rule for us, another for them,' people muttered. (They had been muttering it since Dominic Cummings' lockdown jaunt to Barnard Castle, but that didn't affect the poll ratings: Barnard Castle was another Great Escape.) This was followed by 'Partygate', a series of revelations about parties held at Number Ten during 2020, while the rest of us were in lockdown. There is genuine and deep public anger about this, especially among people who were unable to visit loved ones marooned in care homes and/or dying of Covid. Partygate has a real feel of a First Big Failure about it.

A Big Split seems to be looming, too. Political parties at the start of their Programme's Pomp are largely united. The 2019 Conservatives were particularly so, purged of Europhiles and proudly acting out their First Story by slaying the EU dragon. However, fault lines are now becoming apparent between versions of the Second Story. The factions can be characterized as Charmers and Strivers. The Charmers, led by Johnson, want to spend money on infrastructure, on levelling up North and South, on green projects, and on creating a 'high-skill, high-wage' economy. The Strivers, who include the authors of *Britannia Unchained* and the former Brexit negotiator, Lord Frost, want to spend as little money as possible on anything.

What will be the Slow Stranglers of the Programme? Right now, the most powerful one is sleaze: 'one rule for us…' Inflation, combined with continuing austerity if the Strivers win the battle, is waiting in the wings. Europhiles hope that some aspect of Brexit will play a role; possibly the continuing muddle over the Irish border, or possibly a simple resurgent sense of our European identity thanks to the horrendous story that is unfolding in Ukraine as I write this.

And the Body-blow? History has a habit of springing surprises. All we know is that it will come.

Populist 'Brexit' Nationalism

Leader (eventually): Boris Johnson
Core Policies: Hard Brexit, Culture War, (for Charmers) levelling up
Crucible Groups: Bruges Group, ERG
Action Groups: Anti-Federalist League, Vote Leave, Leave.eu
Sacred Texts: Margaret Thatcher's Bruges Speech, (for Strivers) *Britannia Unchained*
Heroes: Workington Man
Villains: The liberal metropolitan elite, the BBC, experts, 'woke' students/commentators, immigrants
Arch-Villain: the European Commission, 'Brussels'
Significant Influence: Cameron promises referendum in 2013
First Taste of Power: 2016 Referendum
Great Endorsement: 2019 Christmas election
Cultural Endorsement: The Conservative-supporting press
Counterblasts: Banksy's 'EU flag' mural, Global Citizen
Crowning Glory (delayed): Reaching the finals of Euro 2020
Great Escapes: Early reaction to Covid-19, boasts re test and trace
Big Wins: Quitting EU, Vaccine rollout
First Big Failure: ? Owen Paterson affair/'Partygate'
Big Split: Charmers vs. Strivers
Body-blow: ?
Slow Stranglers: Sleaze? Inflation? Problems with Brexit?

The Next Big Thing?

At some time, a new Programme will arise. What form will it take? It is a core principle of this book that the answer is 'nobody knows'. Political Programmes emerge out of the coming together of the pressing concerns of a specific moment and new thinking in some area of modelling how the world works or in believing how it should work. Before that time, it is impossible to know exactly what those concerns or developments will be.

Hence, again, the analogy with art and entrepreneurship, where new ideas are forged with passion by their creators, then pushed out into a world which is initially puzzled by them. If (and only if) these new creations are timely, does the world grow to understand and then embrace them. Hence, also, my quote from St Augustine at the start of the book. Novelty, by definition, means something not yet imagined (or imagined, but not realistically crafted). That is why Political Programmes have that "Yes!" factor. "Of course!" "Why didn't we think of that?"

Despite this radical uncertainty, I can't help making a guess at what The Next Big Thing might be, even though, unlike the previous chapters, based on historical material, this will be a leap in the dark.

My guess is that the next Political Programme will be about the return of Civic Values in general, and concern about the Climate Emergency in particular. Combining these two, I shall call it 'Sustainable Citizenship'.

The civics first. Government would be seen again as a necessary, complex and admirable skill. The post-1979 narrative of vibrant, creative private enterprise contrasted with destructive, nest-feathering government has become dangerously dated. While an age-old cry, it was given an intellectual boost by the economic model known as Public Choice Theory in the 1980s. Since then, Public Choice has, like most theories, turned out to contain some truth but to tell a very partial story. The new Programme would replace its narrative with something broader and more nuanced, where public and private coexist and get on with doing what they do best. We would be reminded that the market can fail, and has, catastrophically in the case of Climate, and that public, state-provided goods and state-protected common resources are an essential part of a decent, civilized society.

Of course, the correction of market failures, the protection of shared resources and the provision of quality public goods cost money. The Leader would have to get voters on board with this expenditure, by convincing them that the spend represents good value. (Any good business person knows that customers look for value, not cheapness.) The Programme's ministers would then have to ensure that it *was* good value. They cannot be wasteful.

The main burden of the increased taxation needed for these would have to fall on the better off ('progressive taxation', in the economists' terminology) – exactly how would be a matter for the Crucible Group. But everyone apart from the poorest would end up having to pay more. The availability of genuinely excellent public goods should go some way to reassuring people of the rightness of this. 'Yes, I am paying more tax, but look at the new hospital in the town!' Welcomed by the sick as a resource, the hospital would also be a source of pride to the healthy. 'We do things properly round here. We look after people who need it.' An ethos of public service would be voiced and valued again.

This ethos would extend to government itself. Our leaders would be citizens, too, with duties and responsibilities. One of these would be simple competence; another fearlessness – it *would* tackle the big issues. A third, and arguably most important, would be telling the truth.

Our world is awash with outright lies, on the Internet and in state media in countries like Russia (are our own perfect?) Some people say we live in a 'post-truth society'. There is no such thing, of course, only post-truth anarchy, which history shows is soon followed by post-truth tyranny. Despite this, truth isn't a primary concern for Populist Nationalists, for whom other things, such as mass emotions and loyalty to the flag, matter more. The new Programme would see things differently, and have an ethic of truthfulness at its core, alongside that of public service.

The truthfulness campaign would begin in government itself. Anyone in office found to have deceived the public in any way, by outright misstatements or by omission, would be sacked. The administration would be honest with the public. 'This is a difficult issue. We are working on the best solution. This is where we have got to so far.' Broader moves to ensure truthfulness in media would be required. This would have to be done carefully, so that truth-seeking journalists were protected from big money but prurient muck-raking was discouraged. Such a line is difficult to draw – which is precisely why we need smart, thoughtful, skilled government.

The policy area on which this new Programme would concentrate most would be the Climate Emergency. This has been pushed into the background by the terrifying events in Ukraine, but has not gone away.

Greenness requires government spending and might lead to lower or even no growth in GDP (though I suspect that effect would be temporary: over time, human ingenuity will create economic growth in new, sustainable ways.) This would be another job for the Leader: convincing the public that this was regrettable but unavoidable. 'Yes, economic growth has flattened out right now, but our grandchildren will inherit a habitable world.'

There is a long queue of Villains for the Programme's First Story. People in public life who tell or spread lies. Polluters, their investors and their advocates in the media and politics. Wealthy tax-evaders. However, a full-on Political Programme needs a strong Second Story, and Second Stories need Heroes. Such as? Experts of various kinds: this would be a job for professionals, not lounge-bar amateurs. Social and green entrepreneurs. Public servants motivated by a genuine desire to help others (the empire-builders and nest-featherers would look all the more obvious once a true ethic of public service was expressed and valued). Regulators, no longer seen as nosey and obstructive but as defenders of the public good against greedy, irresponsible 'free-riders'. The best type of journalist, driven by a passion for important truth. Many other people who quietly get on with essential work – especially carers: in the end not even the most generous state can replace the personal touch.

An objection: wouldn't higher taxation discourage green entrepreneurs? Not fatally. Many entrepreneurs are motivated by a desire to make the world a better place (and, yes, to make money as they do so). The taxation they face would have to be higher but not punitive. The Programme would not be a reinvention of Old Labour envy politics.

Another objection, the one that Margaret Thatcher slammed down on that table in the mid-1970s: Hayek's claim that increased government activity inevitably means diminution of liberty. The new Programme would argue back that a Liberal State is not a contradiction in terms, but is an enabler. It creates freedom by giving people, especially the poorest, more life-chances – as TH Green understood back in 1880. Such a state has to watch itself, of course, and guard against slipping into control-freakery – but so does the current, apparently freedom-loving Programme, which has been trying to clamp down on freedom of protest. A Liberal State must remain self-critical.

Part of the New Future could be a focus on citizens' improved wellbeing (another factor that would compensate for temporary economic setbacks). This may sound fanciful, but there is genuine evidence-based work behind the idea. Around 1990, psychology began a serious investigation of what made happy, effective people happy and effective: a Research Programme known as Positive Psychology. To go into its conclusions in depth is beyond the scope of this book, but much of it is laid out in *Happiness, Lessons from a New Science* by economist Lord Richard Layard (which also goes into its political implications). All this material is ready and waiting to be put at the heart of a Political Programme. The ghosts of 1906's New Liberals will be applauding energetically.

The wellbeing agenda ties in with an appeal to family values. Many of us when asked what we want for our children and grandchildren say 'happiness'. Few say 'bigger GDP'. Rather than lectures on 'getting back to basics', families' real needs are better schooling, opportunities for catch-up education in later life, a flourishing NHS, and kind and effective care for the elderly. In other words, quality public goods.

Inclusivity would be another core value, which would increase general wellbeing. Citizenship is for everyone.

Citizenship can also ripple out beyond the nation state. My sense is that a critical mass of young people around the world are looking in horror at the unpleasant, aggressive nationalists in power in so many countries – then going back to their computers and chatting or gaming with people from all round the world. Encouraging citizenship at home, the Programme would also be proudly internationalist in outlook.

Youth itself might be another aspect of the Programme's appeal. As with all Programmes, there are new voices waiting to be heard.

What might be carried forward from the old Programme? I suspect that Johnsonian technophilia would live on. However much we cut down on car journeys or make our gardens more bee-friendly, the key to a sustainable global future is technology: the brightest minds coming up with brilliant new ideas. The underlying research behind this has – and always had – to be paid for largely by government, as the commercial paybacks are too distant or may not even exist at all.

There is a vibrant Culture waiting to endorse such a Programme, just as *The Lark Ascending* was waiting for Stanley Baldwin, the Beatles for Harold Wilson, and *Captain Corelli*, Britpop and the Spice Girls for Tony Blair. Young people, in particular, are passionate about justice and about the environment (at the other end of the age range, environmentalist Sir David Attenborough is regularly cited as one of our 'National Treasures'). Even business has joined in: Corporate Social Responsibility is finally being taken seriously, as organizations realize that if they are seen as social/environmental Villains, the brightest young people won't want to work for them and the rest of us will be wary of their products.

Sacred texts? There are exciting new economists to read, such as Kate Raworth, Thomas Piketty, Ha-Joon Chang, Carlota Perez and Mariana Mazzucato. On specifically green issues, there is plenty of material. Which is best? I am particularly impressed by the work of the Stockholm Resilience Centre. The Centre's scientists have discovered nine 'boundaries': tipping points that if crossed are likely to throw the entire ecosystem into catastrophic disequilibrium. These don't just relate to greenhouse gases, but biodiversity, ocean acidification, land use, availability of fresh water and pollution of various kinds on land, at sea and in the air.

Nine Giants. Time for a Green Beveridge Report!

What about the Leader? This would need to be a conviction politician. Think Lloyd George (as Chancellor and as War Leader), Churchill (as War Leader), Attlee, Bevan, Thatcher, Blair at his best, or (for all his faults) Farage. They would be passionate believers in the cause, brave standers-up to public opinion (later, they would lead it), superb communicators and would rather die than U-turn on Core Policies.

Which party (if any, of course) would create and host the new Programme?

Labour seems the most likely candidate. Increased government activity and expenditure, with higher, progressive taxation, are much more in their spirit than in that of Conservatism (though taxation was high and progressive under Fifties Conservatives). The Green New Deal, first mooted in the UK back in 2008 by the New Economics Foundation, has been adopted by Labour – albeit eleven years after its publication.

The Conservatives? Johnson has been 'greening' the party, for which he deserves credit. In a way, stopping climate change is the ultimate Conservative policy. Our countryside is at the heart of our national identity – back to Burke again! – and substantial climate change will wreck it. However, a recent survey showed that 15% of Tory MPs still believe climate change to be a 'myth'. The authors of *Britannia Unchained* saw green taxes as a pointless state-as-Villain imposition on its Heroic grafters.

Citizenship, too, is more of a left-leaning notion: Conservatives prefer to see us as economic agents and loyal subjects. The Conservative Party is a master of self-reinvention, but having just reinvented itself rightwards, another shift, even more radical and in the opposite direction, looks a tall order.

The Lib Dems? My sense is that they are moving back away from their flirtation with purely economic Liberalism to something more in line with the Rainbow Circle, Keynes and Beveridge. If so, they are well placed to play a big part in creating a new progressive Programme.

But maybe the most powerful change agent would come from outside the Big Three. Young people I speak to about politics often say that they consider all the main parties to be out of touch but that they would vote Green. The Greens' time may come sooner than we think, at least in terms of getting one hand on the levers of power. This is most likely to come as part of a Progressive Alliance. If such an Alliance is created, it must have its own agreed Worldview and Action Plan, forged by all Alliance members in a serious, argumentative Crucible Group. A Worldview and Action Plan cobbled together after an election will not be robust enough.

The call to act on Climate transcends old loyalties, however: North and

South, young fans of Greta Thunberg and old people pausing to think of their grandchildren, Workington and Islington…

The material in this chapter might sound idealistic, but Political Programmes are idealistic. That's why people champion them, argue passionately for them, and, in the silence of the voting booth, put their X against them with a smile and a flourish.

But, of course, none of this chapter may become reality. Unlike the rest of this book, it is only a personal guess (and, I admit, a hope).

The Next Big Thing (Maybe...)

Big New Idea: Sustainable Citizenship

Core Policies: Create public goods, protect common resources, tackle the Climate Emergency, tell the truth

Carried forward: Focus on technology

Leader: A conviction politician

Crucible Group: Form one!

Sacred Texts: The Green Beveridge Report (not yet written)

Heroes: Experts, public servants (at all levels), informed regulators, genuinely green entrepreneurs, serious journalists, carers

Cultural Endorsements: Anything featuring David Attenborough

Villains: Environmental abusers and their apologists, militant nationalists, tax evaders, people who deceive the public

Gaining Significant Influence: Yet to happen – as is everything else

Big Battles: With many organizations that create, facilitate or benefit from pollution, and their lobbyists/apologists

Slow Stranglers: (?) Higher poorly-targeted taxes, inept regulation, no clear early wins

And meanwhile...

After that peek at things (possibly) to come, I'd like to end to end this book with a look at where we now in the political cycle.

The Populist 'Brexit' Nationalism Programme has already hit choppy waters. 'One rule for them, another for us' is a particularly damaging notion to a populist Programme, where the core appeal is that the leaders are like the ordinary man or woman in the street (unlike that devious, snooty liberal elite). Ambitious, idealistic Conservatives should do whatever it takes to release the grip of this Strangler.

However, the waters aren't *that* choppy, as no alternative Big New Idea seems currently to be on offer, either of the kind I suggested in the last chapter, or of any other. The most common complaint about the Labour Party in the middle of 2022 is that people don't know what it stands for.

Immediately after the Great Endorsement of their rival, this was understandable. Traumatized, post-Waterloo Labour needed time to sit down and ask itself exactly that question: 'What do we stand for?' A level-headed leader at such a time is a huge advantage, and Sir Kier Starmer fitted that bill nicely. But he feels to many to be a transitional figure who steadies the platform so that a full-on Political Programme can later base itself on it. To do this is a fine achievement – and maybe he is still to hit his stride, like another 'Sir': Henry Campbell-Bannerman in the early 1900s.

But things move on. The Labour Party's – or, looking wider,

progressive politics' – Time of Ashes cannot go on for ever. At some point, a Phoenix must arise. Labour only needs to look at its own history to see that Pomps don't necessarily last for long.

An ambitious and angry group of politicians and intellectuals must get together and start a Crucible Group. They must come up with a Big New Idea with compelling Models, Values, Stories and Core Policies grouped round it.

Maybe I'm wrong, but I don't see this happening right now. Political Programmes take time to build, to put down intellectual and political roots, to make mistakes, to learn. Fifties Conservatives were debating The Industrial Charter four years before coming to office. Their next generation founded the Centre for Policy Studies five years before Mrs Thatcher's first electoral victory. Arguably, the Crucible Group for 1945 Socialism formed in 1931. Where are the shoots of real future change, right now? There is a danger that we will drift into a time like the early 1990s, when an old Programme was limping along but there was no sense of a vibrant alternative developing – and all the time the rainforest shrinks, the seas heat up and the poor remain poor.

Advocates of the Green New Deal will say that it is The Next Big Thing. It has certainly gained traction in the Labour Party, but is it at the heart of the party? Other groups may claim that they are the vanguard of change: Extinction Rebellion, Black Lives Matter. These are powerful voices, but outside the mainstream. A Big New Idea will raise a standard around which all such movements can gather, along with more conventional voters. It will act as a magnet, drawing them together and focusing their energies.

Eager Brexiters will disagree with my 'limping along' picture. They will argue that their project, of realigning the British economy away from Europe to the world's emerging markets, is not in trouble but has just begun. Brexiters who dislike Johnson will compare him to Eden, who won a Great Endorsement for Fifties Conservatism but ended up handing leadership over to a stronger spirit who turned out to be the real Leader of the Programme.

However, voters don't seem very excited by this project. The Brexit debate was largely won on the promise of less foreign interference in our lives and more money for the domestic NHS, not on the promise of more globalization. In other words, the Programme's First Story was much more compelling than its Second – about which a Big Split seems in the process of developing, between the Charmers and the Strivers.

And even that First Story is now under threat, thanks to the current nightmare in Ukraine. The arch-villain of the Programme's First Story was Brussels and its bureaucrats. We are now being reminded that there are much, much darker forces out there. The horror, felt by many, that Putin's invasion could happen *in Europe* has been intense. It is clear that only by acting together can Europe's free nations have any effect at all on what is going on. The hesitancy to criticize Russia shown by non-European nations such as China, the UAE and India is worrying: these were going to be the new, trade-driven friends of global Britain.

Brexiters will say that they aren't anti-Europe, just anti-EU. They will point out that it is their opponents on the Corbynite left who are against another European institution, NATO. True, but their hard Brexit was anti-European, deliberately downgrading the importance of trade with Europe. And at a deeper level, pushy nationalism – theirs and everyone else's – has suddenly started to appear a totally inadequate, and indeed immoral, mindset in a world full of nuclear weapons. Vladimir Putin is a model Populist Nationalist.

On a more specific level, Britain's tardy response to the issue of visas for Ukrainian refugees is showing that the Brexiter Nationalist Story is beginning to ring false. The pubic really wants to help these people. To insert a personal anecdote, my wife and I recently took goods to a pick-up point in our town where local bus drivers were taking a van-load of supplies to Ukraine. There was a real buzz there, a powerful sense of taking right action, whatever the cost. *That* is the sense that drives Political Programmes.

The contrasting governmental insistence on making refugees from the conflict go through a complex visa procedure is not an administrative blip but a logical, natural expression of the current Programme's Worldview. Home Secretary Priti Patel has been fiercely criticized for the UK's response, but she is only doing what the electorate told her to do in 2019. She is expressing the Will of the People – as it was then.

Things have moved on. They always do. We need an alternative that reflects this. We need a Next Big Thing, an original Political Programme that has fresh, deeply-thought-through solutions to current and emerging problems, and that stirs voters' hearts and minds so that they once again say "Yes!" and feel that politics matters.

Just 'not being the current lot' won't cut it. Nor should it. Politics is for the bright and the brave.

Ten Quick Tips for the Ambitious

Here are ten key points for anyone seeking to create a Political Programme.

1. Don't Triangulate, Innovate
A Big New Idea is based round a new way of looking at the world, a new set of priorities. Your job is to impassion people, and you won't do this by simply rebadging or recombining old stuff.

2. Start with a Brilliant Crucible Group
Assemble a diverse group of the brightest and best and thrash out your Worldview and Core Policies. Cast the net wide, way beyond just your mates in the party. The Rainbow Circle that created New Liberalism included academics, journalists and Socialists.

3. Form an Action Group
This is more likely to be party-centric. But welcome mavericks. Dominic Cummings helped the Brexiters to victory in 2016/19.

4. Tell your Stories
Think of those tribal elders entrancing their young around a fire on a starlit night. What is the evil dragon and how will we slay it? What New Future will we build once it is slain, and how will we do this?

5. Ride the Wave
Does the spirit of these Stories chime with positive, upbeat trends in culture (especially popular culture)? Enjoy this and use it!

6. Have the Right Leader

This person must be energetic, energizing and attractive to many voters. They must be a true believer in the Big New Idea, and must be PM material. However, remember Lloyd George in 1918/22: your Leader is not running for President.

7. Be Thick-Skinned

Remember, too, that Sir Keith Joseph, arguably the leading intellectual force behind Thatcherism, was nicknamed 'the mad monk' by his colleagues in the early 1970s.

8. Be Patient. Very, very Patient.

The Zeitgeist moves in a mysterious way. If your Big New Idea is strong and you keep fighting for it, its time should come.
The Brexiters began their campaign in the late 1980s; they achieved their Great Endorsement in 2019.

9. Understand your Internal Rivals' Neediness

If you have truly (and finally!) caught the public mood, you offer your party colleagues what they crave most: office. Once you convince them this is true, they (or enough of them) will bury their old hatchets and rally round you. In the early 1960s, Labour stopped squabbling and came together (enough) to support White Heat.

10. Do not Compromise any Elements of your Big New Idea for Quick Wins as you Gain Influence

This is a particular danger for an Aspirant Programme offered a Taste of Power in a coalition. The 'Orange Book' Liberals paid the ultimate electoral price by agreeing to raise student loans.

Appendices

Appendix A. The Status of my Model

Having talked earlier about the philosophy of science, I can't help but wonder about the philosophical status of the model I present in the book. Is it a 'fact'? A 'law'?

No. No model can perfectly capture all reality's shades and subtleties. Models in the 'hard' sciences like Physics and Chemistry aspire to this goal and can get pretty close. Maybe they can even achieve it: no exception has yet been found to the Periodic Table of the Elements. But in human and social affairs, models have to find a humbler place in what is known as Thorngate's Impostulate. This is a triangle where one corner is *Accuracy*, another is *Simplicity*, and the third is breadth of application (or *'Generalizability'*).

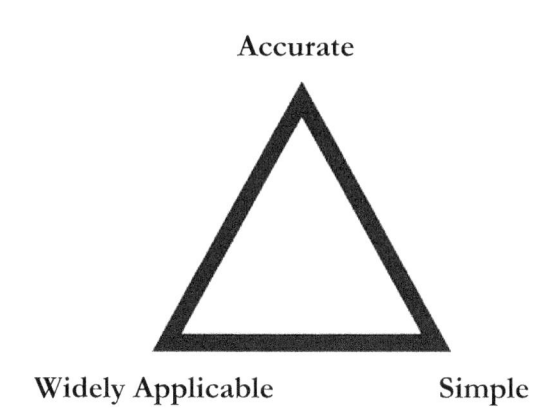

Accurate

Widely Applicable   **Simple**

If you want perfection in one direction, there will be trade-offs in one or two of the others. The most ambitious models go for a high level of accuracy plus one of the other two desiderata, breadth and simplicity.

Karl Marx, for example, believed his model to be totally accurate and reckoned it was universally generalizable, applying to all of human history. Simple? No: *Das Kapital* contains 300,000 words of dense prose. An Ordinance Survey map, by contrast, is scrupulously accurate and delightfully simple to use – but not generalizable at all; it is only a model of the one particular chunk of the UK that it covers.

Some social scientists regard the Impostulate as a cop-out, but I think it is how knowledge about complex, human systems works. I believe that the model I have presented in this book is pretty accurate, works in a very wide range of situations and is easy to use. In the best Lakatosian tradition, I believe it will predict the course of the current Political Programme – that it will slowly run out of legitimacy and energy, but that it won't be replaced until someone comes along with a genuinely Big New Idea. I believe it will be a useful guide for those people seeking to replace the current Programme – but also a reminder that they, too, will only have a limited period of real power. The wheel of fortune never stops turning.

Appendix B: The Big New Ideas

These are presented with the year of their first accession to power (their year of Great Endorsement, where different, is shown in brackets). Aspirant Programmes from the 1970s and 2010s are in italics.

1905 (1906)
New Liberalism. The poorest people in the UK are trapped in poverty. We will set up a German-style welfare system to enable them to escape this and lead fulfilling lives. We will pay for it with income and land taxes, not import tariffs, as Free Trade creates wealth.

1916
The Knock-out Blow. Germany represents absolute evil, so the War must be fought to the end and won, whatever the price. To do this requires massive state intervention in the economy and ultimate political control of the military.

1918
A fit Country for Heroes to live in. Lloyd George's charismatic leadership. Continued Liberal reforms at home, including finally sorting the Irish question. (?)Germany will be punished for the Great War.

1922 (1924)
Tranquillity. Let the nation unite, under Baldwin's gentlemanly, avuncular leadership. Avoiding extremism, we will quietly get on with wealth-creation. Internationally, we will work towards creating a more peaceful world through diplomacy, but there will be as little meddling in foreign affairs as possible.

1940 (1945)

1945 Socialism. The state owns the 'commanding heights of the economy' and provides free education and healthcare. Fair shares for all (hence the need for continued rationing.) The fighting/working man and woman are the new Heroes.

1951 (1955)

Fifties 'One Nation' Conservatism. The Welfare State provides a safety net but no more: people must be free to pursue their own economic success. Old rules: no tinkering with the existing social structure or traditional values (family, patriotism, church etc.)

1964 (1966)

White Heat. Modernization of economy and society via planning, science and technology, meritocracy, social liberalization, removal of the 'old boy network'.

1970

Heathism. *(pre-U-turns) Join EC. 'Selsdon' economic freedom.*

1974

The Social Contract. *Unions, CBI and government to co-run Britain. Prices and Incomes policy.*

1979 (1983)

Thatcherism. Take on the trade unions. No more Keynesian tinkering with levels of demand in the economy: 'supply-side' economics will help businesses thrive and create employment. Promote enterprise, free markets, low tax, small state – at home and abroad (especially in Eastern Europe). Patriotism.

1997

New Labour. An inclusive community where individuals are free to live as they choose. Women's and minority rights asserted. 'Third Way' economy: increased expenditure on public goods to be provided by a mixture of state and private capital.

2010

The Big Society *Decentralize power to responsible citizens – nudge them if they need directing. Socially liberal. The debt must be paid off – austerity, continued cuts in government spending, is the only way to do that.*

2016 (2019)

Populist 'Brexit' Nationalism. Hard Brexit – as great a distance between ourselves and Europe as possible. A free trading 'Global Britain', with low taxation, low levels of regulation and a small state. Culture wars: take power from 'liberal, metropolitan elite'. Level up North and South.

And maybe…

20??

Sustainable Citizenship. Government has a key and unique role in promoting the public good. Solving the Climate Emergency is the biggest public good of all. Taxation will have to rise to pay for this, and must be 'progressive' to retain a sense of fairness. Thinking must be international as well as national. There will be a stress on Wellbeing. An ethic of public service will return.

Appendix C: Glossary

Action Group. A small, self-defined group that meets to drive a Political Programme from being a purely intellectual entity to actually having political power. (Compare with 'Crucible Group'.)

Action Plan. A list of Core Policies, prioritized in order of urgency.

Ashes (Time of). The period after a political party has had its latest Programme obliterated (= that Programme's Waterloo). The Programme is dead, but the party lives on, albeit traumatized. After a healing period, a Phoenix (a new Political Programme) should arise from the Ashes, the exception (so far) being the Liberal defeat of 1922.

Aspirant Political Programme. A set of Models, Values, Stories and Core Policies, grouped around a Big New Idea, which has *not* achieved a Great Endorsement from the electorate (i.e. it has not been Politically Successful).

Big Battle. A struggle with a major interest group whose power is so entrenched that it can only be taken on during a Programme's Pomp.

Big New Idea. The essence of a Programme's originality and purpose, summed up in a simple sentence, word or phrase. The analogy with an 'elevator pitch' in business is helpful.

Big Split. A fundamental disagreement between two sections of a political party, resulting in the establishment of publicly warring factions.

Big Win. The successful rollout of a Core Policy. Can also be a highly successful piece of 'Normal Politics' (qv).

Body-blow. An event that seriously and permanently damages the credibility of an administration, by destroying one of its key supports. This can be a course of action that goes badly wrong and shows that the Worldview of the Programme is now wrong, or it can be a U-turn on a major Policy. A key moment in the Degeneration of a Programme.

'Bright Ideas'. Often not-very-bright ideas that administrations come up with during their Degenerating phase, to try and whoop up public enthusiasm. Some work better than others, but voters want deeper thought and more radical action.

Canon. A small collection of texts that are of substantial influence on the founders of a Programme.

Carried forward (of a policy). An aspect of one Programme that is also adopted by a subsequent one. Example: the policy of the Welfare State, carried forward from 1945 Socialism to Fifties Conservatism.

Central Stories. The two narratives at the heart of a Political Programme. The First Story, Slaying the Dragon, is about how negative, damaging things will be swept away. The Second Story tells how a great New Future will be Built once this has happened.

Clamping Down. Actions by an undemocratic regime, where it responds to policy failures by violently stifling criticism.

Core Policies. The policies that a Political Programme considers essential. These must be carried out. Major deviations from them (see 'U-turns') are fatal.

Counterblast. A flowering of artistic creativity during a Programme's Pomp, which expresses a radically different Worldview to that of the Programme.

Crowning Glory. A spontaneous national celebration of some kind, which (roughly) coincides in time with a Programme's Great Endorsement. It is felt by many people as a moral version of the Programme's electoral triumph. 'We're on the right track (at last)!'

Crucible Group. A small, self-defined group that meets to develop the core Models, Values, Stories and Policies of a Programme. (Compare with 'Action Group'.)

Cultural Endorsement. A flowering of artistic creativity around the time of a Programme's Great Endorsement or during its Pomp, which shares and expresses that Programme's Worldview (or much of it).

Degenerating Political Programme. A Programme that has fallen behind the pace of change, and is now making more and more mistakes. It may have received (or is just about to receive) a Body-blow, be in the grip of Slow Stranglers, and may be (or be about to be) riven by a Big Split.

Democratic Revolution. When a new Political Programme achieves full power via a Great Endorsement.

Dethronement The moment when a rival Programme gets its First Taste of Power. The dethroned Programme's advocates will be dismissive of this, and will still think they can fight back. Usually, but not always, they are wrong.

Dissolution. The process whereby a once-mighty Political Programme falls apart after its replacement has triumphed in a Great Endorsement.

<u>First Big Failure</u>. A major policy error by a Programme, usually late in its Pomp, which begins to erode public confidence in the Programme. "We still love you, but..." (contrast with 'Great Escape' and 'Body-blow'.)

<u>First Taste of Power.</u> The moment a Programme becomes responsible (in part, at least) for policy. This can be in coalition, in government but with a tiny majority, or in government with a slightly bigger majority but under a barrage of sustained criticism. The Programme is still 'on approval' from the voters; later it will either be rejected by them or be rewarded with a Great Endorsement.

<u>Foil.</u> The 'number two' to a Leader. Not necessarily with a formal title like Deputy PM, but the person with whom they work in tandem to create and/or deliver the Programme.

<u>Founder.</u> A member of a Programme's Crucible or Action Groups.

<u>Great Endorsement.</u> A substantial electoral victory. 100 seats or more ideally. Certainly 60 or more. It is the achievement of this that turns an Aspirant Political Programme into a fully-fledged one.

<u>Great Escape.</u> A major policy error by a Programme early in its Pomp, which the public forgives at the time, because it still believes strongly in the Programme and shares its Worldview.

<u>Leader.</u> The driving individual force of a Political Programme – not necessarily (but often) from the very start.

<u>Limping Along.</u> What a Degenerating Political Programme does.

<u>Normal Politics.</u> Policies that are not Core, but which are created in response to unexpected events that happen after the Programme has

achieved power. Examples: Harold Macmillan's decolonization of Africa, Margaret Thatcher's Poll Tax. Politically, these do not carry the same weight as Core Politics. Normal policies can be reversed, and should be if they clearly aren't working.

<u>Palace Revolution</u>. A change of Political Programme caused by personnel and ideological changes within a ruling party. In democracies, these still need endorsement at the ballot box (during wartime, this endorsement has to wait).

<u>Political Programme</u>. A Politically Successful set of Models, Values, Stories and Core Policies, grouped around a Big New Idea.

<u>Politically Successful</u>. A Programme is Politically Successful if it achieves a Great Endorsement (qv).

<u>Pomp</u>. The period after a Programme has received a Great Endorsement. During this time, the Programme is 'Teflon-coated', and has the time and space to realize its Action Plan.

<u>Replacement Leader</u>. A leader who takes over after the fall of a full-on Political Programme Leader. Examples: Alec Douglas-Home, John Major, Gordon Brown.

<u>Representative Democracy</u>. Our current system, with general elections every five years or so, which return MPs, one for each constituency. Contrasted on one side with ideas like 'direct democracy', which means regular referenda on major issues, and on the other with authoritarianism (rigged elections, autocratic leaders, dissent stifled).

<u>Sacred Text.</u> A text that has been of substantial influence on the Founders of a Programme.

Significant Influence. The moment when the Leader of an aspirant Political Programme achieves a position of influence, usually as Leader of the Opposition.

Slogan. An eye-catching way of drawing attention to what is special about a Programme. (By contrast, the Big New Idea is what actually is special.)

Slow Strangler. A problem that comes up again and again (and again and again), but which a Programme seems helpless to solve.

Three Fates. Metaphor for the three inevitable forces that cause the Degeneration of a Political Programme. These are a Body-blow, Slow Strangler(s) and a Big Spilt.

Triumphalism. An unnecessary, hubristic 'rubbing the old enemy's face in it' at the start of a Programme's Pomp.

U-turn. The abandonment or reversal of a Core Policy.

Villain. In a Programme's First Story, an individual or organization serving the malign force from which the country has to be freed.

Waterloo. The moment when a Programme knows it is truly defeated and begins to fall apart.

Worldview. A set of Models of how the world works, Values (how the world should work) and two Central Stories, which together form the explanatory core of a Political Programme.

Zeitgeist. A deep swell of public opinion on 'big' political and moral matters.

Appendix D: UK General Election Results, 1906 - 2019

Year	Winner	Leader	Maj	
1906	Liberals	Henry Campbell-Bannerman	129	Great Endorsement of New Liberalism
1910	(Liberals)	HH Asquith	-	Minority government
1910	(Liberals)	HH Asquith	-	Minority government
1918	Coalition	David Lloyd George	283	Great Endorsement of 2nd LG administration
1922	Cons	Andrew Bonar Law	74	First Taste of Power for Tranquillity
1923	(Lab)	Ramsay Macdonald	-	Minority gov't. Aspirant PP fails to take off.
1924	Cons	Stanley Baldwin	210	Great Endorsement for Tranquillity
1929	(Lab)	Ramsay Macdonald	-	Minority gov't. Second attempt by Aspirant PP, also fails
1931	National	Ramsay Macdonald	492	Huge underlying Cons majority makes this a continuation of the Tranquillity Programme
1935	National	Stanley Baldwin	242	As above
1945	Lab	Clement Attlee	146	Great Endorsement of 1945 Socialism
1950	Lab	Clement Attlee	5	
1951	Cons	Winston Churchill	17	First Taste of Power for Fifties Conservatism
1955	Cons	Anthony Eden	60	Great Endorsement of Fifties Conservatism

1959	Cons	Harold Macmillan	100	
1964	Lab	Harold Wilson	4	First Taste of Power for White Heat
1966	Lab	Harold Wilson	98	Great Endorsement for White Heat
1970	Cons	Ted Heath	30	Dethronement of White Heat
1974	(Lab)	Harold Wilson	-	Minority government
1974	Lab	Harold Wilson	3	First Taste of Power for Aspirant Social Contract
1979	Cons	Margaret Thatcher	43	First Taste of Power for Thatcherism
1983	Cons	Margaret Thatcher	144	Great Endorsement of Thatcherism
1987	Cons	Margaret Thatcher	102	
1992	Cons	John Major	21	
1997	Lab	Tony Blair	179	Great Endorsement of New Labour
2001	Lab	Tony Blair	167	
2005	Lab	Tony Blair	66	
2010	Coalition	David Cameron	78	… but no overall majority for any party (Cons 307, Lab 258, LD 57, Rest 28)
2015	Cons	David Cameron	12	
2017	(Cons)	Theresa May	-	Minority government
2019	Cons	Boris Johnson	80	Great Endorsement of Populist 'Brexit' Nat'ism

Acknowledgements

I hope you have enjoyed this book and found it stimulating. Any comments or thoughts would be hugely appreciated. My email is chris@chriswest.info.

Rather than clog the book up with footnotes, I have put references on a special page on my website, www.chriswest.info

Sources differ on precise size of electoral majorities. Some calculations include the Speaker; others don't. Independent candidates often muddy the waters. I have used the figures that I have seen most often cited. The most-debatable figure is that for Lloyd George's Coalition in 1918: my source here is the invaluable *British Electoral Facts, 1832 – 2012*.

Books are always team efforts. Special thanks to…

Gervas Huxley at Bristol University, who went through an earlier draft with great thoroughness and expertise. We've also had loads of phone conversations, which have been invaluable.

Graham Michelli, who suggested the concept of the a 'big idea' as the key to serious electoral victory.

My wife, Rayna, and my daughter, Imogen, for long conversations on various topics in this book over the dinner table or on car journeys.

Printed in Great Britain
by Amazon